FURNITURE
YOU CAN MAKE

By the editors of *Sunset Books* and *Sunset Magazine*

Lane Books • Menlo Park, California

Edited by Donald W. Vandervort

Design and Layout : Lawrence A. Laukhuf

Illustrations: Alyson Smith

Diagrams : Vernon Koski, Alyson Smith, Joe Seney

Cover: Table and chair plans on pages 23
and 67. Chair design: Rick Morrall.
Photograph by Ells Marugg.
Design consultant: John Flack.

FIRST PRINTING NOVEMBER 1971

CONTENTS

INDOOR FURNITURE

OUTDOOR FURNITURE

BUILDING & FINISHING TIPS

INDOOR FURNITURE

Making a piece of furniture that will endure, that is pleasing to look at, and that will complement the other furniture in your home, should call forth your best efforts in craftsmanship and design. With planning, patience, foresight, and a fair amount of skill in using basic tools, you'll find that making furniture can be a pleasant and profitable outlet for your creativity. If furniture making is new to you, follow the plans on the following pages closely. Although some were developed by home craftsmen, most are by professionals—furniture designers and builders, architects and designers, decorators, and cabinet makers. Those readers who have an eye for design and experience in making furniture might use these plans simply as ideas for designing more personalized pieces. If you take this road, be sure the piece you design appears graceful and pleasingly proportioned, yet is at the same time tough enough to withstand everyday use. Before you begin the actual construction of a piece of furniture, it's a good idea to look through the entire book, paying particular attention to the special section in the back on building and finishing tips.

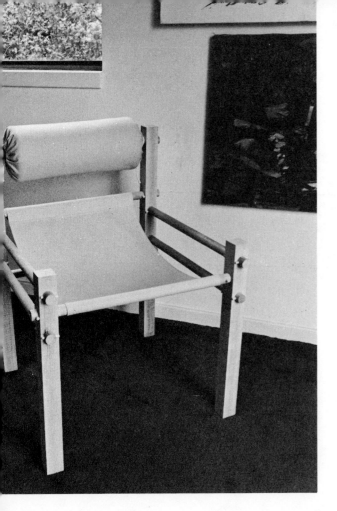

Lounging chair

The interesting appearance of this lounge chair makes it a natural conversation piece in any living room. It is made from birch lumber and doweling, plus some cotton chair duck. The cylindrical back rest is of a polyurethane foam roll, purchased at an upholstery shop. This chair could also be made of fir or hardwood, with leather seating.

To make the inexpensive version shown, you will need about 9 feet of birch 2 by 2; 18 feet of 1-inch doweling; 5 feet of ¼-inch doweling; 4½ feet of chair duck (29 inches wide); and a 6-inch-diameter, 17-inch-long polyurethane foam roll (you can cut it to the proper length with a bread knife).

Cut and drill all the pieces to size (see illustration). Before covering the foam roll with chair duck, push the back-supporting dowel through it, and stitch a ½-inch loop along each side for drawstrings. Stitch fabric ends together around foam roll and gather tight around the dowel with drawstring. Sew a 1-inch hem along both long edges of the seat fabric, and double-stitch a 4-inch loop in each of the ends for the dowels to pass through (be sure seat will be at proper tension).

Assemble the chair sides with dowels and ¼-inch dowel pegs. Finish with a stain or clear finish before sliding chair duck in place.

Design: Donald Wm. MacDonald, AIA.

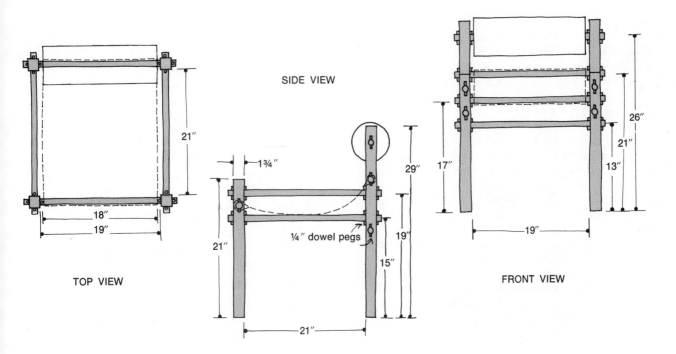

TOP VIEW SIDE VIEW FRONT VIEW

Chair and couch that match

For the home craftsman eager to build major living room pieces, here is a sofa and lounge chair set. The design is basically the same in the two units; only the width of the seat changes. Both couch and chair are made from ³/₄-inch and 1¹/₈-inch plywood (obtainable at any major lumberyard). Cushions are added for comfort—you can make your own from dense polyurethane foam, or have them made in an upholstery shop.

To cut the plywood, a power saw will come in very handy. See techniques of working with plywood, page 84. Plywood members are fastened together with 2 by 2-inch fir or birch bars and ¹/₄-inch machine bolts (see illustration). Countersink washers about ¹/₂-inch into the supporting bars. Bolt heads should show from the outside.

The wood can be finished naturally (plywood edges need to be treated, see page 85); you can paint it a bright color; or you might pad the plywood members and cover them with upholstery fabric matching the cushions (use screw-in snaps to attach fabric).
Design: Donald Wm. MacDonald, AIA.

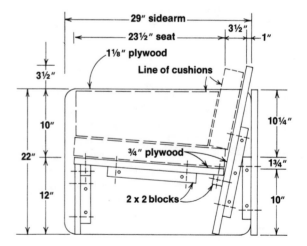

SECTION VIEW

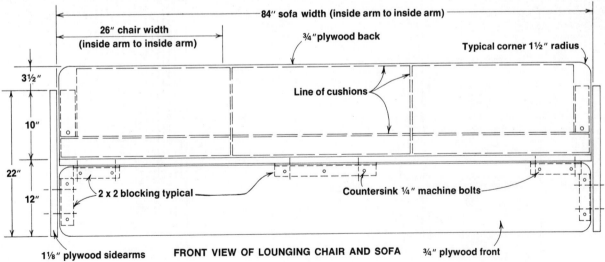

84″ sofa width (inside arm to inside arm)

26″ chair width
(inside arm to inside arm)

¾″ plywood back

Typical corner 1½″ radius

3½″

Line of cushions

10″

22″

12″

2 x 2 blocking typical

Countersink ¼″ machine bolts

1⅛″ plywood sidearms

FRONT VIEW OF LOUNGING CHAIR AND SOFA

¾″ plywood front

Bolt-together dining chair

Designing a dining chair that is sturdy, good looking, comfortable, and easy to make is a sizable chore for many home craftsmen. But here is a well-planned chair that you can easily build, particularly if you have a table saw, a jig or saber saw, and a power sander.

Use square-edged fir or birch (have it milled at the lumberyard). For one chair, you will need about 25 feet of 1 by 2 lumber, 18 feet of 1 by 6 lumber, 3 feet of 2 by 2 lumber, and 7 feet of 2 by 4 lumber. In addition, you will need six $\frac{1}{4}$-inch threaded rods $15\frac{3}{4}$ inches long, and 12 nuts and washers.

Cut out all pieces as shown in plan. To avoid having to readjust saw settings, cut all identically-sized pieces at the same time. During the cutting operation, contour the seat to the form you wish. To assemble chair, drill all $\frac{1}{4}$-inch holes (a pattern for drilling holes may come in handy), insert rods, and tighten down the nuts.

Design: Donald Wm. MacDonald, AIA.

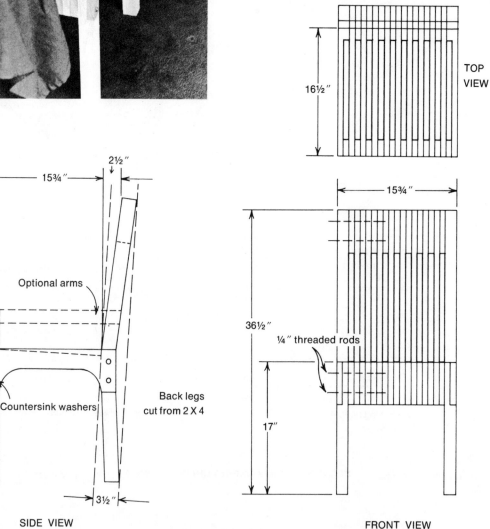

TOP VIEW

16½"

2½"

15¾"

Optional arms

Back legs cut from 2 X 4

Countersink washers

3½"

SIDE VIEW

15¾"

36½"

¼" threaded rods

17"

FRONT VIEW

Dining chairs from plywood

Here is a dining chair made from ³/₄-inch plywood. You can easily modify the basic design in any of a number of ways. The photo above shows the basic construction of the chair, but you should relieve the "heavy" appearance of the chair by cutting slots in the back and sides or by adding colorful pads (as shown in the sketch). Decide for yourself on the size and shape of the slots—they should complement each other to balance the design. Those in the chair sides will, besides being decorative, provide hand-holds for lifting or moving.

Although the chair appears to be made entirely from plywood, beneath the seat are four 2 by 2-inch birch bars bolted to the panels with ¹/₄-inch machine bolts. Two bars support the seat and two support the back. Heads of the bolts show on the outside of the chair; washers and nuts are countersunk in the birch bars.

Depending upon the number of chairs you need to go around your dining table, determine the number of 4 by 8-foot sheets of ³/₄-inch plywood required—about one per chair. Cut out the pieces as shown in the plan (see tips on working with plywood, page 84). Upon completion, chairs can either be stained or painted. Design: Donald Wm. MacDonald, AIA.

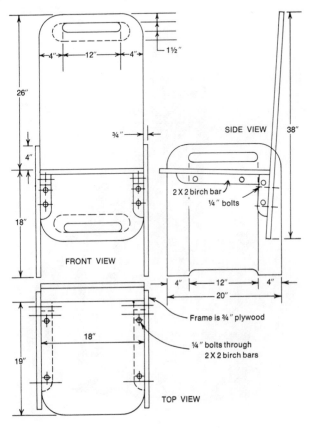

Super beanbag...giant pillow

Here are a couple of fun-to-use projects that are guaranteed to liven up the decor of any room.

Super beanbag. Take a running leap and see what happens—any way you land, these jumbo beanbags are comfortable to sit, lie, or curl up in. They adjust to your body to form a chair that's so comfortable you'll be reluctant to get up—and they're easy to make.

For the football-shaped striped bag, you will need 4½ yards of 45-inch-wide heavy, machine-washable cotton. The larger, floppier, pear-shaped version requires 5¾ yards of 45-inch fabric. The lining or inner casing (to permit the outer covering to be removed for periodic washing) is a bag of identical size and shape, made of unbleached muslin. You will also need two zippers for each bag (one for the inner casing, one for the outer bag): 12-inch ones for the

football shape, 22-inch zippers for the pear shape. And you'll need about 14 pounds of styrene foam pellets for filling.

Both beanbags are constructed in the same manner. Cut six side panels and six top and bottom sections. Stitch the long sides of side panels together (½-inch seam allowance). For reinforcement against bounces and jumps, lap both seam allowances to one side and top stitch (or make flat felled seams). Continue sewing all panels together until all six are attached in tube fashion, open at both ends.

Sew top in small end of bag, easing all edges. Attach zipper to center seam of base, sewing securely across both ends of tape to prevent stuffing leakage. Stitch bottom in larger end of tube to form the base. Follow same procedure for muslin lining, but use a ⅝-inch seam for easy fit.

Slip muslin casing inside outer bag, and roll back both tops together in preparation for filling. A large funnel of heavy paper will direct the lightweight, statically-charged styrene foam into the bag (fill it about ⅔ full). Close the zippers, and you're ready to relax.

BEAN BAGS are filled ⅔ full with granulated styrene foam pellets.

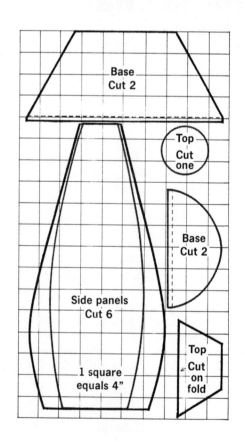

Base
Cut 2

Top
Cut
one

Base
Cut 2

Side panels
Cut 6

1 square
equals 4"

Top
Cut
on
fold

BEAN BAGS *are versatile. As a lounge, plop one on the floor and fall on top; as a chair, sit down and wiggle around to form a backrest. Pear-shaped version (right) is relaxing for the weary.*

The giant pillow is an item that grandma referred to as a hassock, ottoman, or pouf. There was always one or two in front of the fireplace; the children spent hours rolling around on them. They all but disappeared in the early part of this century, but a good thing dies hard.

Here's a modern version you can make with ease. Unlike pillows you purchase, these have a removable casing to allow for cleaning.

Fabric selection is the most important step when making these pillows. Choose a close-weave fabric with a bold design. Your pillows can vary in size. Three to four yards of either 45 or 54-inch-wide fabric will work well. Hold up a doubled piece of fabric to judge the approximate size of your finished pillow.

Also purchase a piece of muslin the same length and width as your fabric, a dress-type zipper at least 36 inches long, and some shredded foam. (A 36 by 48-inch pillow will need about 9 pounds of foam.)

To assemble the inner pillow, fold the muslin in two and cut along the fold (otherwise the pillow will stuff unevenly). Machine-stitch muslin together $5/8$-inch from the edges leaving at least a 24-inch opening on one side. Trim corners and turn right side out.

To stuff the pillow, tear the cellophane bag of shredded foam along one side and place inside the muslin covering *before* emptying the bag. It is wise to fill the pillow outdoors because loose bits of foam tend to stick to furniture and rugs. Wear old clothes. When pillows are full and firm, close the opening with a blind stitch.

For the casing, fold the fabric in two and cut along the fold. With outer sides together, stitch along one side and put in the zipper on this seam following instructions on the zipper package. *With the zipper open,* stitch up the other three sides. Trim corners and turn right side out through the zipper opening.

Stuff the muslin pillow in the case and close the zipper. If the pillow becomes soiled, just remove the case and clean.

Glass-topped coffee table

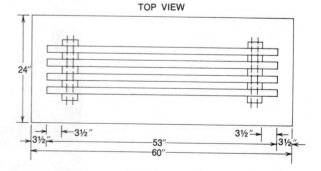

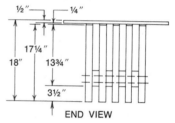

½ " ¼ "

17¼ "

18" 13¾ "

3½ "

END VIEW

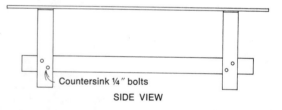

Countersink ¼" bolts

SIDE VIEW

TOP VIEW

24"

3½"

3½" 53" 3½" 3½"

60"

These coffee tables are easy to build—just cut the pieces, bolt them together, and add the top. Their design is adaptable to almost any decor, depending upon the top you select. The tops illustrated are glass, but you can use terrazzo, marble, plywood, plastic, or butcher-block— all of which can be purchased in a form ready to lay directly on your table.

Because the base is such a "beefy" structure, thick top materials look best. If you choose glass, one-inch-thick plate glass is preferred, but you can use sizes as thin as ½-inch. If you plan to use plywood, buy the ¾-inch size (remember edges need to be faced, see page 85). Laminated butcher-block tops can be purchased in various sizes at most lumberyards.

To make the table shown above, you will need about 32 feet of standard 2 by 4 birch; four ¼-inch brass or chrome machine bolts 13½ inches long; ten ½-inch by 3½-inch rubber pads cut from reversed—that is, rubber side up—indoor-outdoor carpet (these are to keep glass from sliding on leg tops); white glue to attach the pads; and material for the top.

Mark, cut, and drill all pieces, countersinking for washers. It is best to use a square to accurately mark holes for drilling.

Design: Donald Wm. MacDonald, AIA.

...and two variations

Table shown below requires about 26 feet of fir or birch 2 by 4 lumber. Unlike the one on opposite page, shelf beneath the top runs full length of the top. Also, since only four legs support the structure, less lumber is required. Otherwise, the plan is basically the same. You will need four $\frac{1}{4}$-inch brass or chrome machine bolts (or threaded rods) $13\frac{1}{2}$-inches long, and four $1\frac{1}{2}$ by $3\frac{1}{2}$-inch rubber pads. Mark, cut, and drill pieces; then bolt them together, countersinking washers into the outside of the legs.

Square-shaped table (at left) requires about 14 feet of standard 1 by 6 fir or birch. Mark and cut double cross-lap joints in horizontal members (see plan below). If you plan to add a transparent top, be especially careful to cut these joints precisely. Mark and cut all pieces to length and drill the holes. Use eight $\frac{1}{4}$-inch brass or chrome machine bolts $4\frac{1}{2}$ inches long and countersink washers. A small rubber cleat under each leg will help table level itself.

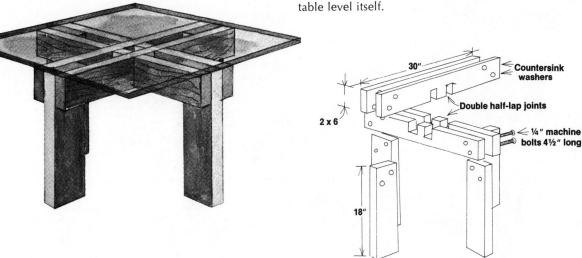

Countersink washers

30"

Double half-lap joints

2 x 6

$\frac{1}{4}$" machine bolts $4\frac{1}{2}$" long

18"

Angle iron-and-walnut coffee table

The entire framework of this attractive table is iron (right angle and T-bar) painted black. Top, end pieces, and drawers are solid walnut finished in natural shade with bar varnish.

This 5-foot-long table is unusually sturdy, and all wood parts can be easily detached to simplify any future refinishing. The double-ended drawers slide both ways on their metal supports, making them accessible from either side of the table.

Unless you own (or can borrow) welding equipment, you will need to have the metal frames made at an iron works, welding shop, or garage. Prices vary greatly, so get several estimates.

With the frame assembled, build the drawers to fit fairly loosely in their angle-iron and T-bar runners. Bottom edges serve as pulls, so no hardware is needed. Wax the metal runners for smooth drawer operation.

If desired, you can fit a $1/4$ to $1/2$-inch-thick end panel to either end of the table. Make the two pieces of a height to match your drawer faces and either wedge them into place as diagrammed with small pieces of scrap wood, or bolt them to the angle-iron legs and top rails.

The top is made of several walnut planks, edge-glued together—to form a single piece. Narrow pieces of hardwood glued together as in a chopping block—or a single piece of $3/4$-inch plywood with edges trimmed—would serve well. The top is secured by several screws inserted from below through holes drilled in the metal frame.

Paint the metal frame and finish all wood parts *before* final assembly.

Design: Robert F. Wallace.

HANDY DRAWERS slide on angle-iron runners; they are accessible from either side of the table.

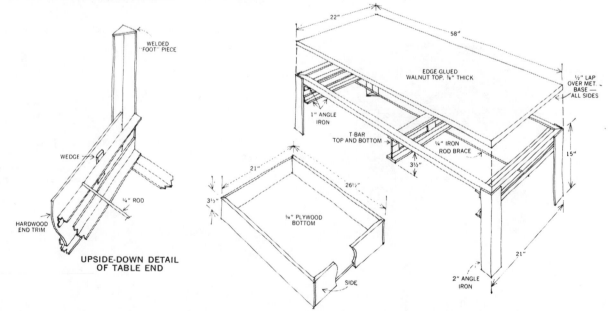

WELDED "FOOT" PIECE

WEDGE

HARDWOOD END TRIM

$1/4$" ROD

UPSIDE-DOWN DETAIL OF TABLE END

22"

58"

EDGE-GLUED WALNUT TOP, $3/8$" THICK

$1/2$" LAP OVER MET. BASE — ALL SIDES

1" ANGLE IRON

T-BAR TOP AND BOTTOM

$1/4$" IRON ROD BRACE

$3\frac{1}{2}$"

15"

21"

$26\frac{1}{2}$"

$3\frac{1}{2}$"

$1/4$" PLYWOOD BOTTOM

SIDE

2" ANGLE IRON

21"

See-through end table

This attractive piece of acrylic plastic furniture serves as both an end table and a magazine rack. It is totally transparent—you can see inside from any angle. The two inner shelves have a curved front lip and are slightly sloped downward toward the back, making it easy to slide magazines into place.

The table is made from ¼-inch plastic. Sides are 13 by 18 inches. The back is 18 inches high and 13½ inches wide (the extra ½-inch will overlap the sides). Top is 13¼ by 13½ inches (the extra ½-inch overlaps the sides, the extra ¼-inch overlaps the back). These fittings must all be exact. Shelves are 13 inches wide and *about* 16 inches long—cut to length after bending the front curve.

All edges must be sanded before gluing the panels together (see page 86).

To bend shelves, you will need to heat the plastic with a strip heater (page 87), then bend it in a home-made jig like the one illustrated below. After bending the front of each shelf, place it face down on the table saw (put paper under plastic for protection) and cut at an 80° angle about 13 inches from the bent portion. Remember to decide upon the length of the shelf before making the cut.

Assemble the top, back, and one side first. Then, glue the two shelves in place (making sure they are square and even before gluing). The back of the top shelf is 9 inches down from the tabletop; the back of the lower shelf is 15½ inches from the tabletop. Check the second side for fit before gluing it in place.

Design: Donald W. Vandervort.

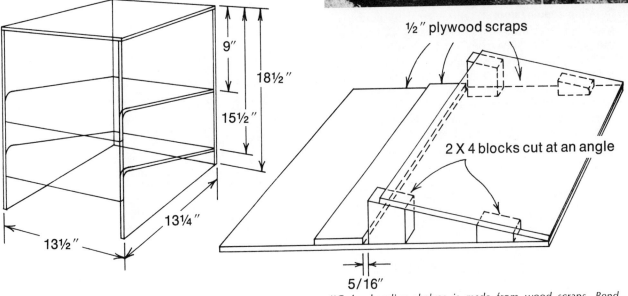

½" plywood scraps

2 X 4 blocks cut at an angle

5/16"

JIG for bending shelves is made from wood scraps. Bend plastic with heated side away from wood.

9"

18½"

15½"

13¼"

13½"

Small tables for grouping

Parsons tables can be functional and attractive additions to almost any type of room. Because of their modular shape, they are either grouped or used individually. The tables can be stained and finished to match other wooden pieces in the house; they may be painted in a variety of colors; or the tops can be covered with plastic laminate (see page 87). If you use exterior-grade plywood and apply a durable finish, the tables can be used outdoors.

Tops are ¾-inch A-D plywood. Either birch or fir can be used for framing pieces. Legs measure 2½ by 2½ by 17¼ inches; side rails are 13-inch lengths of 1 by 2. Beneath the top, butting against and mortised into the top of each leg, are short pieces of 1 by 2. Use a backsaw—*not* a hacksaw— and chisel to cut mortise after drilling out excess wood.

Glue and screw all pieces together using 2-inch screws. Attach mortise-pin to leg (making sure leg will sit squarely), attach legs and side rails to top (overlapping plywood ¼-inch to allow for edge facing), and add pieces abutting inside corners.

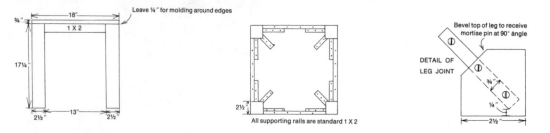

The simple table/stool at right is great for people on the move. These little tables can be easily taken apart to form a flat stack of plywood. To make one, all you need is two 18-inch-square pieces and one 13-inch-square of ¾-inch plywood, four 3-inch metal corner brackets, and a few ¾-inch screws. Simply make a ¾-inch-wide, 9-inch-long cut along the centerline of the two 18-inch boards, slide them together, and attach the third board to the top with brackets. Sand rough edges and paint with a high-gloss enamel.

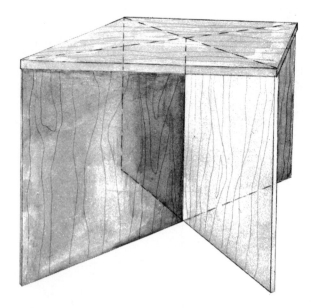

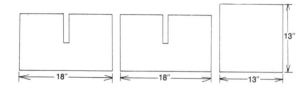

CUT OUT PIECES, slide them together, and fasten the top with metal corner brackets and screws.

A three-sided table in the form of an equilateral triangle (modified to remove pointed ends) can be used by itself or in combination with other units to create larger tables of interesting geometric shapes. Two tables form a diamond (or rhombus), three a trapezoid, four a triangle or parallelogram, six a complete hexagon (see photo at right).

The top of each table is beveled along all edges of one face at 45° to form miter joints with legs and side strips; legs are beveled 45° at one end and side strips are beveled 45° along one edge. In addition, 30° angles are notched in the tops of legs in order to receive side strips. The lower shelf is dadoed ⅛-inch into legs.

Because several angle-cuts are required, a power saw would be extremely useful. With careful marking and a plane, you can make the long 45° bevels by hand. Use a backsaw and a chisel to cut the 30° notches.

If you plan to make several of the units, make a cardboard template of the top and bottom shelves to save time measuring.

The tables shown here were made of solid Philippine mahogany. They were glued and nailed, stained, and then varnished with polyurethane. If you make the units out of plywood, remember to treat the edges (see page 85).

Design: Clifford M. Hickman.

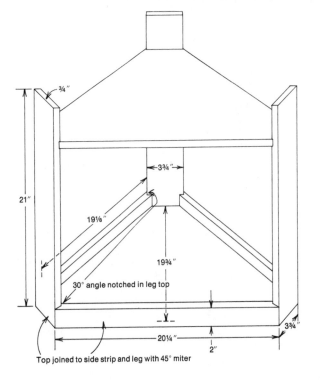

USED SINGLY or grouped, triangular tables form interesting geometric shapes both indoors and out.

¾"
21"
3¾"
←3¾"→
19⅛"
19¾"
30° angle notched in leg top
20¼"
2"
3¾"
Top joined to side strip and leg with 45° miter

17

Convertible table for coffee or dining

In a small house, summer cabin, or space-hungry apartment, you may not have room for all the furniture your comfort requires. Here is a table that allows you to transform your living room into a dining room and back again in a matter of seconds. You can use it as a coffee table, dining table, or buffet.

In the up position the table is 25 inches high. In the low position, the table is less than 15 inches above the floor.

The basic frame is made from standard 2 by 2 lumber. Join rails with either mortise-and-tenon or dowel joints

(see page 89). The top in the illustration is made from standard 1 by 6 lumber (actual dimension $^3/_4$ by $5^1/_2$ inches) spaced $^1/_4$-inch apart and faced around all edges with standard 1 by 4. You can make the top out of almost any type of wood—$^3/_4$-inch plywood is a good choice.

Upper leg sections, attached by piano hinges, fold away under the top when the table is in the low position. For further building and finishing tips, see pages 82-95.

Design: Richard Dennis.

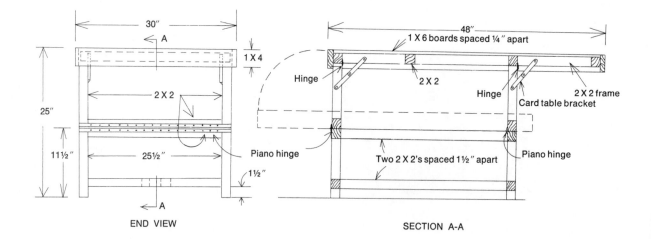

END VIEW

SECTION A-A

Indoor-outdoor table

Designed with a flavor of Early American style, this trestle table can be used for dining either indoors or out (it seats six), or used as a roomy desk. It is easy to make and can be disassembled easily for moving or storage.

The table is made from one sheet of ¾-inch plywood (except pegs for securing legs and supports). Type of plywood is up to you—depending upon whether you plan a natural finish, stain, or paint. Whatever the intended finish, plywood should be top grade. If you don't plan to paint it, remember plywood edges will have to be treated (see page 85). To give the tabletop an appearance of thickness, you can miter a 1¼ by ½-inch edge-strip around it.

The table consists of a top, two sides, three horizontal supports (two at the top and one in the center), and 12 wooden pegs. The top is 54 by 36 inches, standing 30 inches from the floor. Metal corner brackets fasten the top to its trestle base inside the end pieces. Horizontal supports are inserted through slots in end pieces and secured with 3-inch-long pegs of ¾-inch-diameter doweling.

To make the table, first cut the 4 by 8-foot sheet of plywood into three workable sections (as shown in the sketch). From these, you can then cut the particular pieces—carefully mark them, allowing for saw kerfs. You will need a saber saw, or else a drill and keyhole saw to cut the slots in the end pieces. Pattern for the end boards is optional—instead of the "step" pattern shown, you can round angles or cut special shapes. For further information on working with plywood, see page 84.

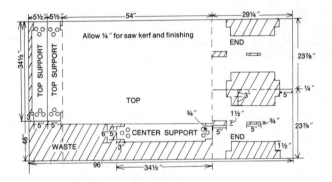

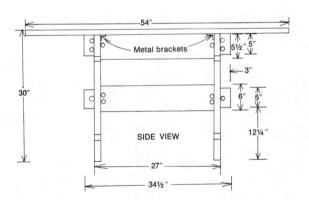

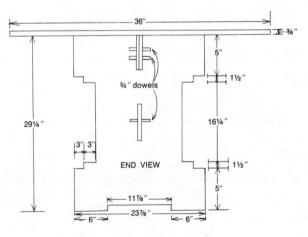

Maple table...heavy and handsome

This table—used both for informal dining and as an all-purpose work surface—can be a pleasant and useful addition to a kitchen. The top is basically a block of 1³/₈-inch-thick laminated maple, about 3 feet wide and 7 feet long. Lumberyards and building supply dealers can order tabletops like this for you, or you can make your own (see page 90).

Ash was specified by the designer for the 1 by 2¹/₂-inch hardwood edge and for the legs and supports, but any attractively-grained hardwood will do.

To cover the screws (which should be deeply countersunk), use ready-made plugs or doweling .

Before finishing the table, lightly round all edges with sandpaper. Oil top and edge of table with several coats of paraffin oil, or use a Danish or plastic oil finish. Use plastic oil on rest of framework. Sand between applications with carbide paper to achieve a mellow, satiny finish.

Design: Robert Hersey, AIA.

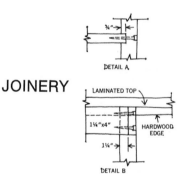

JOINERY

TOP VIEW. An ash frame is mitered and glued around the maple-block top.

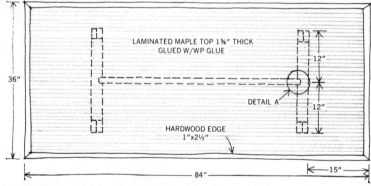

SIDE VIEW. Center rails, at top and bottom, notch into cross bars.

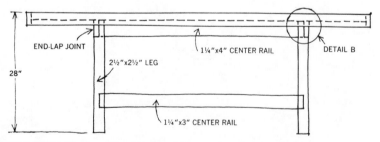

END VIEW. Plugs cover flathead screws.

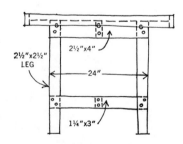

This inlaid table is willow

Willow wood finished with a fruit-wood stain has a mellow look in this handsomely-grained dining room table. Three and one-half feet wide, seven and one-quarter feet long, it seats 8 to 10 people comfortably.

Two-inch-thick willow planks (selected in random widths for esthetics and economy) are edge-glued (see page 90) and supported by cast aluminum legs. Three of the planks used are $9^{1}/_2$ inches wide; one is $7^{3}/_4$ inches wide; and one is $5^{3}/_4$ inches. Decorative rosewood butterflies are inset $^{1}/_2$-inch deep.

If you choose not to join and inlay the planks yourself, a cabinet-maker can do the work, and you can finish the tabletop and add legs. The planks can be factory glued; you can rout or chisel out the recesses for the butterfly inlays or eliminate them entirely as they serve no structural purpose.

Cast aluminum legs, purchased at a lawn furniture store, were painted black. If the legs are a bit short for dining, raise the table to the proper height by inserting a 2-inch-thick triangular block of wood between each leg and the tabletop. Glue wood blocks to underside of table and screw legs in place.

To finish the table, sand with fine sandpaper; stain; and apply two coats of varnish, rubbing the surface down with fine steel wool after each coat.

Willow weighs about two-thirds as much as oak and costs about the same. If your retail lumber store does not have it in stock, they can order it for you.

Design: Ted Van Doorn.

2-inch wood block

Cast aluminum leg

SCREW each cast aluminum leg into a 2-inch-thick triangular wood block and glue blocks to underside of table. This will raise top to comfortable height.

Table and bench set seats twelve

Trim workmanship and a high-gloss finish makes this maple-top dining set appropriate in any setting—indoors or out. Designed for a beach house, the large table and set of six two-seater benches will seat 12.

Tabletop and bench seats are random-width strips of 1¼-inch-thick maple, doweled and glued (see page 90). Legs and rails are clear pine, held together with pegs and bolts rather than screws—so that the sections can be dismantled easily.

All pieces should be smoothed with a scraper and carefully sanded before finish. For a long-wearing surface, apply a sealing coat of thinned clear shellac, then two coats of a mixture of turpentine and clear varnish, followed by three additional coats of unthinned varnish. Sand surface between coats.

If the set pictured seems too large, note that all linear dimensions at both table and benches can easily be scaled down.

Design: William Ross.

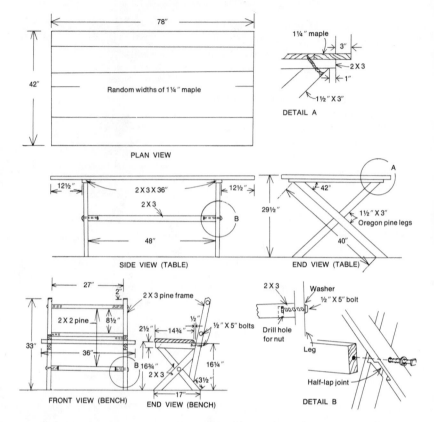

Clean lines, generous size

This large dining room table (see front cover) combines the clean lines of a Parsons table with the functional appearance of a chopping block. A short-cut lamination process produces the chopping block look and saves on time, cost, and effort.

The table is made of vertical-grain fir, milled at the lumberyard to remove rounded edges. The top has a $3/4$-inch plywood base covered with 1 by 2-inch strips of fir attached with screws. Countersink the screws $1/4$-inch. Coat the 1 by 2's liberally with glue (bottom and sides) and screw them onto the base, using expanding clamps to hold them together as you work. If a board warps sideways, apply clamps at points of warpage and drive nails from the underside to hold the strips parallel. Cover screws with fir plugs cut from scraps with a plug-cutter bit.

With a band or circular saw, trim the excess wood at the ends and one side. Screw a 2 by 4 frame to the underside and a second frame of 2 by 4's around the table's perimeter. With a handsaw, notch the corners to receive the 4 by 4 legs. Chisel rough edges to right angles.

Clamp legs into notches. Mark and drill $1/2$-inch holes for 9-inch dowels. Remove legs, if necessary, to drill holes deeper.

Use a belt sander for smoothing the tabletop. After fine sanding, finish with oil or varnish.

COUNTERSUNK SCREWS and glue hold strips to plywood base.

DOWELS anchor legs to notched top. Last plug on surface is decorative.

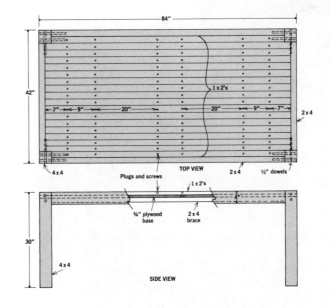

Pedestal table

Seating eight is no problem with this oversized round table. The laminated tabletop stands solidly on its pedestal base—offering plenty of elbow and knee space. It's pleasing to the eye, inexpensive, and easy to make.

To make it, you will need about 200 linear feet of clear, square-cornered 2 by 2's; a quart of resin glue; a box of 8-penny finish nails; a 28-gallon paper drum; forty 28-inch lengths of 1 by 2; a box of ¾-inch tacks; and a 20-inch square of ¾-inch plywood.

No clamps are needed in the table's construction—it's glued together in a very simple way. Assemble the 66-inch-diameter top by working from the middle out, edge-gluing each 2 by 2 progressively and adding a nail every 8 inches. Work on a flat surface. You can use a yardstick, as shown on page 90, to mark the cutting line around the top. Be sure not to nail along this line.

When all pieces are glued, cut along the marked circle with a saber saw, band saw, or coping saw (see "Cutting a Circular Tabletop," page 90).

The base is made from a standard 28-gallon paper drum. Measure 28 inches up from floor and cut off remainder (about 2 inches). Cover drum with 1 by 2's notching each about ¼ by 2 inches to fit over metal ring at bottom. Glue each generously and hold in place with ¾-inch carpet tacks (four per slat) from the inside. After about half the drum is covered, place slats loosely around unfinished part to determine whether remaining 1 by 2's will have to be planed or sawn to fit.

Cut the ¾-inch piece of plywood to the inside diameter of barrel and attach to tabletop with several screws. For a large table like this, you may want to brace the top by nailing and gluing a 2 by 2 crosspiece on the underside. Sand well and apply three coats of oil sealer.

Design: Rick Morrall.

BASE SLATS are glued and tacked to a cut-down paper barrel; notch them to fit over metal ring at base. A ³/₄-inch piece of plywood is cut to fit inside diameter of barrel; attach it to tabletop with screws.

Pine table...black walnut inlays

Inlaid black walnut strips make this simple sugar pine table the center of attraction. The round top makes it possible to evenly space a variable number of place settings—up to six. In addition, the legs can be detached easily for moving.

The tabletop is made from 11 lengths of 2 by 6 sugar pine. Rabbet a ¼-inch-wide by ½-inch-deep groove along one edge of each board with a saw or router. Join and cut the top (following directions on page 90). When planks are joined, glue walnut strips in the rabbet grooves. When all glue is dry, sand the top flat in preparation for applying a hard finish.

Underneath the table, two 2 by 6 boards run the diameter, joined in the center by a cross-lap joint and a 3-inch lag bolt (see illustration below). Attach boards to tabletop with metal brackets. Bolt each of the four 2 by 3 legs with two 3-inch machine bolts (countersink washers) four inches from each end of the 2 by 6's (on the right side). Although legs shown in photograph are slightly tapered and set at an angle, those described above are easier to make and more attractive in design. They're also less likely to get under foot.

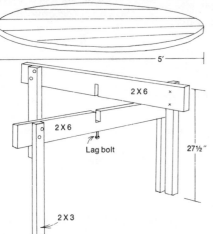

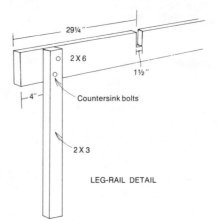

LEG-RAIL DETAIL

How to make simple bookshelves

Bookshelves are about the easiest type of furniture to build, and because almost everyone can use an additional place to park books, a bookshelf is a great project for beginning craftsmen. Too, in economical terms, bookshelves can usually be less expensively constructed than purchased.

When you decide to make your bookshelf, first choose the space it will fill. Would you prefer it against a wall or freestanding as a room divider? If you are really short of space, you might even decide to build it *into* a wall.

Most freestanding bookshelves require support across the back. A 1/4-inch A-D plywood back is one of the best answers to problems of sway and rocking. If you intend to place your bookcase against a wall and would rather see the wall than a plywood back behind the books, the supporting members can be nailed or screwed directly to the wall. The bookshelf shown at the top of the opposite page is solid enough to stand sturdily without back support.

If the bookcase has a back, you can provide support across the back

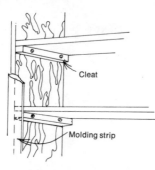
Cleat
Molding strip

of long shelves by using a wooden cleat made of either spare lumber ripped to size or strips of 1/4-round molding. This type of cleat can also be used to support the ends of the shelves. If you don't want the cleats to show from the front, mask them with a face frame or molding strip.

If you don't use a cleat along the back for long shelving, it may be necessary to provide added strength by using upright wood supports at the

span's midpoint or spaced at 1 or 2-foot intervals (a standard 1 by 6 usually works well).

Where cleats would be impractical and the shelf not required to carry a heavy load, all the support needed may be obtained by dadoing the sides of the cabinet and inserting the shelf; the added strength of glue and nails makes a strong bond. Cutting this type of groove requires power tools, and once the shelf is placed, its position can't be changed.

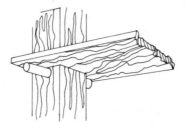

Dowels can be very handy for supporting shelves from the sides. The bookcase on page 28 uses a dowel fitted between two 2 by 3's to support a shelf. If shelf ends are notched,

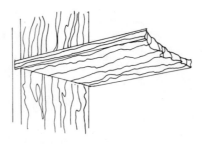

you can build a room-dividing bookcase by cutting a standard 4 by 4 to reach from floor to ceiling (where it is attached with an L-shaped bracket) and running dowels through at varying heights to hold the shelf ends. Or, a back cleat can be combined

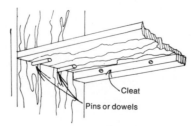
Cleat
Pins or dowels

with pins or dowels on the sides of a bookcase to form a sturdy support.

There are many different types of metal fixtures available for bookshelves. Brackets, braces, and angle irons can be purchased in a wide variety of sizes, shapes, and styles (including ornamental designs) for attaching open shelves to either back or end supports. Metal brackets add strength where a heavy load is to be placed on shelving.

For adjustable shelving—a great way of eliminating waste space—wall standards with notches 1/2-inch apart can be purchased along with special brackets to fit them. They are available either for shelves supported from the sides or from the back. For end support, a pair of the 5/8-inch-wide standards and two brackets for each side of each shelf are needed. For back supports, one pair of wall standards will do, unless the shelves are extra long. Stock lengths of the standards range from 24 to 144 inches. Brackets lock into place.

You can choose almost any wood for bookshelves, provided it can stand the dead weight of the volumes it will hold (average 1 to 3 pounds per running inch of shelf). Commonly used types are 1 by 12-inch fir and particle board and 3/4-inch plywood. Many lumberyards carry 1-inch-thick bookshelf stock that has a rounded front edge. Standard T-1-11 plywood and 2 by 3 lumber are used in two designs shown on the opposite page.

Bookshelf space should be a minimum of 9 inches high and 8 inches deep for books of average size. Larger volumes may require a shelf 12 inches deep and 12 inches high. Width usually depends on the number of books you have to shelve—figure 8 to 10 average-sized books per running foot of shelf. The highest shelf should be no more than 76 inches off the floor.

Designs (opposite page):
Donald Wm. MacDonald, AIA.

Freestanding bookshelf stands sturdily without a back; it is solidly made from 2 by 3 lumber. Construction is simple; all you do is cut the lumber to length, mark and drill holes (countersinking for washers), and bolt it together. It can easily be disassembled when you move. If the dimensions given don't fit the space you wish to fill, you can make minor changes in its size by simply allowing the boards a little more length or else cutting them shorter.

Materials may prove to be relatively expensive: 114 feet of standard fir or birch 2 by 3 and twenty-four $\frac{1}{4}$-inch rods 16$\frac{1}{2}$ inches long (with washers and nuts) are required.

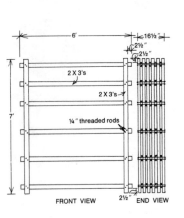

Plywood sections, slipped together, are the basis of this simple bookcase's construction. It has a back, so it should be used against a wall.

Once you have marked and cut out one vertical and one horizontal panel, use them as templates to mark the other panels. All plywood is $\frac{3}{4}$-inch thick. Grade A-A is used for vertical members, since these will be visible from both sides; A-B is used for shelves (best side up). The back is made from A-D since the appearance of only one side is important. Back is nailed to shelves. See additional information on working with plywood, page 84.

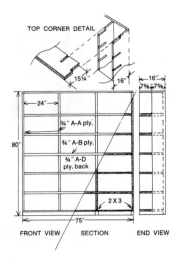

Grooved plywood, called "Texture 1-11", forms dado grooves for shelves to slide into. Plywood is $\frac{5}{8}$-inch thick, grooves are $\frac{3}{8}$-inch wide on 4-inch centers. You can also obtain this plywood with grooves on 2 and 8-inch centers.

Using 2 by 3 lumber, make 4 frames 6 feet 8 inches high and 16 inches in depth. Glue and nail plywood to form boxes inside each 2 by 3 frame (see plan). Be careful not to smear glue where plywood will be exposed on the two outside ends. Shelves can be made to either 16 or 24-inch widths; use $\frac{3}{8}$-inch A-C plywood. See tips on working with plywood, page 84.

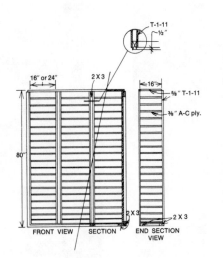

Shelving on rungs

These shelving units are adjustable through use of ladder-like supports. The shelf unit shown at right was constructed of commercially-built ladders fastened to ceiling and wall. The six-foot-long desk surface is made from 1 by 12-inch lumber; two more shelves can be added to convert the piece into a bookcase. This unit was designed by John T. Jacobsen.

The shelves below are supported by 1-inch dowel rungs and fir 2 by 3's. To make this bookcase, you will need about 40 feet of birch 2 by 3, six 1 by 6 shelf boards 85 inches long, and twenty-two 11½-inch lengths of 1-inch doweling.

Measure 12 inches in from each end of each vertical member and mark for a one-inch hole every six inches. Use a square to transfer marks from one 2 by 3 to the next. When drilling holes, be sure to keep the drill straight in order to prevent problems later in aligning dowels. (Also, when tip of drill bit appears through one side of the 2 by 3, turn it over and finish drilling from other side to avoid splitting-out the wood.) Pound dowels into place with a mallet, using white glue for extra strength. Miter a 2 by 3 between each pair of vertical supports (forming two pairs) and lock pairs together with notched horizontal 2 by 3's. Notch shelves to fit, apply stain or clear finish, and attach unit to wall.

SHELVES are supported by rungs. Notch ends of shelving boards to fit snugly between vertical supports. Height of shelves is easily changed. Bookcase can be dismantled.

Wall organizer

All you do to make this simple shelving unit is cut the pieces to size, drill holes, and bolt the sections together. Very few tools are required: a saw (power saw, if you have one) to cut the 3/4-inch plywood pieces and 1 by 1-inch birch-bar connectors, a drill to bore holes through all pieces, and screwdriver and wrench to tighten the bolts. Before cutting out plywood, see tips on working techniques, page 84.

Exact size of the plywood pieces is optional. Width can be 8, 10, or 12 inches; length may be 16, 18, 20, or 24 inches (these dimensions are used in order to make fullest use of 4 by 8-foot plywood sheets). Length of birch bars varies according to width of plywood piece —add 1/2-inch to width.

Units can be cantilevered (see photo), or you can omit a shelf, thus making the modules twice as tall or twice as wide. Attach shelving to wall with metal corner brackets.

Design: Donald Wm. MacDonald, AIA.

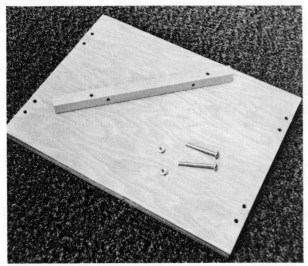

PREDRILL PLYWOOD and 1 by 1-inch birch bars to receive bolts—use 1/4-inch machine bolts.

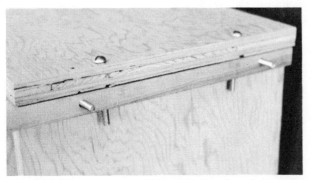

CORNER JOINT is essence of the shelving unit. It is formed by bolting birch bar to the plywood pieces as shown. Shelves can be cantilevered, or made twice as large by leaving out one panel.

Mix-and-match storage modules

Made to any size you desire and stacked together, these cabinets are attractive storage and display pieces for your living room, family room, or bedroom. They can be built to house books, stereo hi-fi equipment, television sets, aquariums, and all sorts of decorative objects. The modules can be used against a wall or freestanding as attractive room dividers (because they are made of heavy 2 by 12 lumber, no rear panel is needed for reinforcing, so you can see right through them).

The two that are shown housing stereo speakers are enclosed at the front by plywood panels cut out to mount the speakers, with 1 by 1 wood strips on the inner sides to permit securing the panels to the cabinets with nails. Speaker cloth then covers all. The interior shelves in the other cabinets are of ¼-inch smoked glass.

The cabinets are easy to build. Pick out the straightest clear softwood planks you can find at your lumberyard (the examples here are redwood). If you don't have a radial-arm saw, it's best to have the lumberyard cut the pieces to the exact lengths desired, because a long plank is heavy and difficult to cut square with other types of saws.

On the side pieces, measure in 2 inches and drill holes 1 inch apart for adjustable metal shelf pins. (Make sure holes are straight across from each other so shelves will sit level.) Sand the flat surfaces before assembling. Then glue and clamp the cabinets together and drill ¾-inch dowel holes in them, as shown in the photo on facing page. Glue and firmly seat softwood dowels of a contrasting color.

To round the corners, draw lines across the top and bottom pieces to give the limits of the curve and draw arcs on the edges of the corners with a small paint can or similar round object to outline the curve. Do the rounding with a rasp or power sander, working with the wood grain.

Design: Rick Morrall.

SIMPLE MODULES stack together to hold books, stereo hi-fi equipment, and other objects. Cabinets can be arranged to serve as a room divider or used against a wall. One houses a television set in the photo at right.

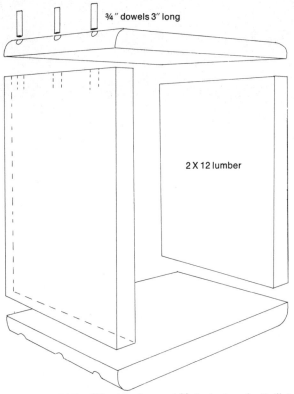

¾″ dowels 3″ long

2 X 12 lumber

ASSEMBLE CABINETS with glue and ³/₄-inch dowels. Drill 3-inch-deep holes and tap dowels in place with mallet.

GLUE AND CLAMP corners of 2 by 12 lumber. Drill and insert ³/₄-inch dowel pins before rounding corners.

USE A RASP or a power sander to round the cabinet's corners. Work downward with wood grain.

Three easy-to-make magazine racks

Everyone knows that magazines tend to gradually eat up all the space on coffee and end tables, pile up in cabinets, and clutter bookcases. For this reason, most people find that they can always use a magazine rack.

The racks shown on these pages are attractive and easy to build. The tall wall-rack (illustration below left) takes up very little space, yet can hold and display a large selection of magazines. The cloth-and-wood

holder (below right) is light and easily carried from room to room. The freestanding rack (opposite page) will hold books as well as magazines and has additional storage space beneath the display rack.

BACK VIEW

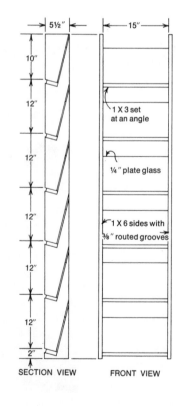

Wall rack stands on two tall lengths of 1 by 6 lumber, routed to receive panels of 1/4-inch plate glass (or acrylic sheet plastic for safety if there are children in the house). Magazines rest on 15-inch-long 1 by 3 boards, dadoed in the tall 1 by 6's at a slight backward angle. These 1 by 3 shelves are spaced 12 inches (on center) apart. The height of the unit is determined by your ceiling height. Use metal corner brackets to attach it to ceiling and wall. Assemble the unit with finishing nails and glue before sliding the glass into place.

Design: Donald Wm. MacDonald, AIA.

Cloth-and-wood holder is made from birch strips, 1/2-inch dowels, and a 4-foot remnant of cloth. The frame can be assembled with butt joints, then nailed and glued. For a sturdier frame, use dowel joints (as shown in sketch). The one shown was finished with clear lacquer.

5½"   15"

10"

12"   1 X 3 set at an angle

12"   ¼" plate glass

12"   1 X 6 sides with ⅜" routed grooves

12"

12"

2"

SECTION VIEW   FRONT VIEW

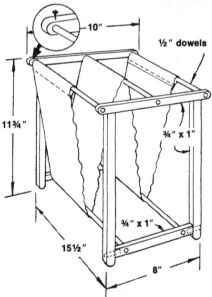

10"   ½" dowels

¾" x 1"

11¾"

¾" x 1"

15½"   8"

32

Freestanding magazine rack has a frame made from 1 by 12-inch lumber. Magazine display holder swivels up on 2 spring-loaded dowel pins (see illustration) to reveal additional magazine storage. Sides are rabbeted into the top, and the ¼-inch plywood back is rabbeted into the frame. Shelves are held by dado joints. (For information on joints, see page 89.) Unit is assembled with glue and finishing nails. It can be finished naturally, stained, or painted.

Design: Albert C. Lechner.

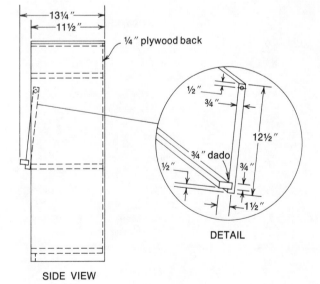

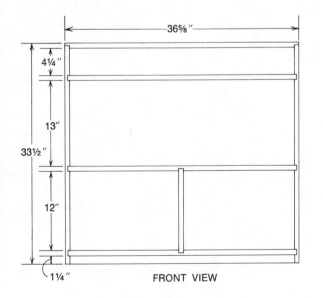

FRONT VIEW

SIDE VIEW

¼" plywood back

DETAIL

Desk and storage with a flair

Practical and economical, this home storage and desk center is an attractive addition to almost any room. The unit has shelves, cabinets, drawers, and a fold-down desk. It's freestanding and demountable.

Here are the basic construction steps: (1) build the five plywood modules plus desk, (2) build the lumber frame, and (3) assemble the plywood modules on the lumber frame and fasten. The unit shown is made from four panels of ⅝-inch exterior DFPA-grade plywood (Medium Density Overlay both sides), and one and one-half panels of ¼-inch B-B interior DFPA-grade plywood (for dividers, backs, and drawer bottoms). You will also need 72 linear feet of 2 by 2 lumber (select grade) and 60 linear feet of 1 by 4 lumber (select grade). For hardware required, see below. To minimize waste, mark lengths of lumber carefully before cutting. Cut 2 by 2 vertical framing to fit ceiling—or shorter if desired. (For detailed information on working with plywood, see pages 84-85.) Assemble plywood box modules first, using glue and countersinking nails.

Design: John D. Bloodgood, AIA, for American Plywood Association.

HARDWARE

Qty.	Description	Use
6 ea.	2" (approx.) cabinet door hinges and screws	Cabinet doors
4	Door pulls	Doors, drawers
2	Magnetic door catches and screws	Cabinet doors
¼ lb.	1" brads	Fasten drawer supports
1	1⅟₁₆"x34" chrome piano hinge and screws	Fasten desk top to desk top section
1 pr.	1½" butt hinges and screws	Desk legs
3	Small screen door hooks and eyes	Latch desk legs, cross member
1 box	6d finishing nails	Fasten plywood box modules, drawers, desk
122 ea.	#8x1¼" ovalhead screws and finish washers	Fasten lumber framing and box modules to framing
2	#8x2" flathead screws	Fasten 2x2 cross piece

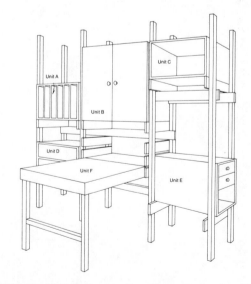

LETTERS CORRESPOND to plan diagrams for the different plywood modules that are shown on the opposite page.

84″ (optional up to 96″)
2 X 2 (8 pieces)
19″ 1 X 4 (16 pieces)
28″ 1 X 4 (2 pieces)
3
4
1
66½″ 1 X 4
55″
30⅞″
11/16″ spacing
15⅛″
2
28⅜″
39″ 1 X 4
1″ overhang

STAIN OR PAINT all framing members and allow to dry thoroughly, then move framing into room for assembly. Pre-drill and screw together all 2 by 2 and 1 by 4 framing members, attaching those marked 1-4 last.

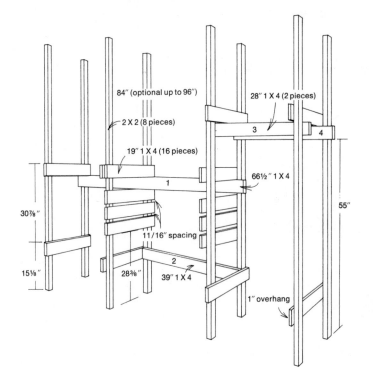

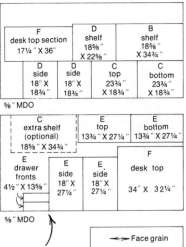

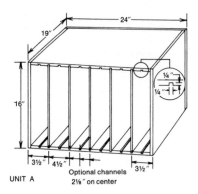

24″
19″
16″
¼″
¼″
3½″
4½″
Optional channels
2⅛″ on center
3½″
UNIT A

UNIT A. Dimensions are same for units A, C, and D—except D is 18 inches high.

36″
19″
4″
32″
4″
UNIT B

UNIT B. Paint before adding hinges, pulls, and magnetic catches.

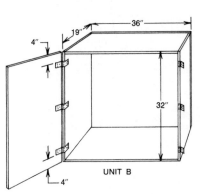

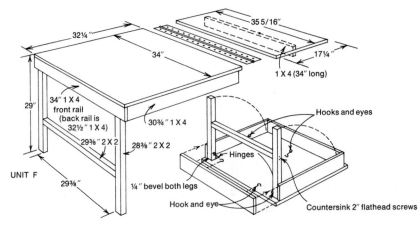

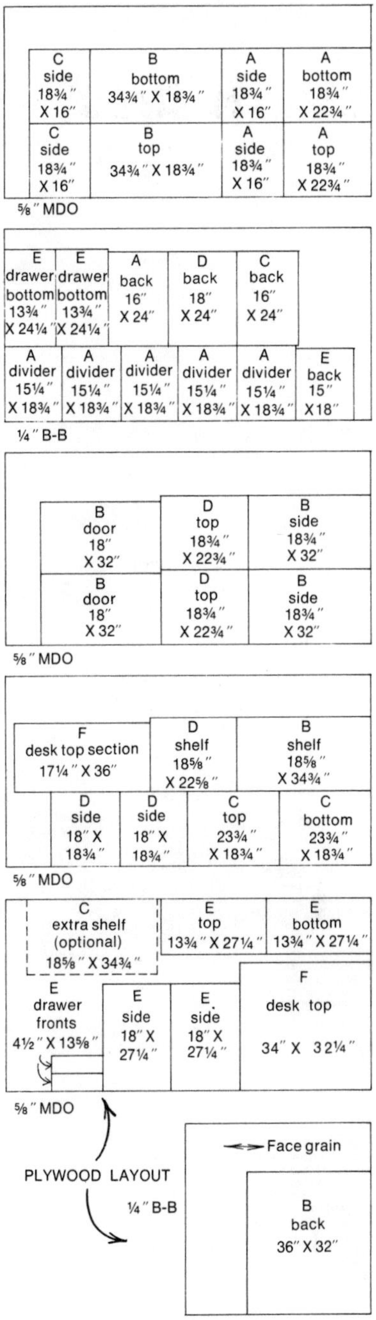

C side 18¾″ X 16″
B bottom 34¾″ X 18¾″
A side 18¾″ X 16″
A bottom 18¾″ X 22¾″
C side 18¾″ X 16″
B top 34¾″ X 18¾″
A side 18¾″ X 16″
A top 18¾″ X 22¾″
⅝″ MDO
E drawer bottom 13¾″ X 24¼″
E drawer bottom 13¾″ X 24¼″
A back 16″ X 24″
D back 18″ X 24″
C back 16″ X 24″
A divider 15¼″ X 18¾″
A divider 15¼″ X 18¾″
A divider 15¼″ X 18¾″
A divider 15¼″ X 18¾″
A divider 15¼″ X 18¾″
E back 15″ X18″
¼″ B-B
B door 18″ X 32″
D top 18¾″ X 22¾″
B side 18¾″ X 32″
B door 18″ X 32″
D top 18¾″ X 22¾″
B side 18¾″ X 32″
⅝″ MDO
F desk top section 17¼″ X 36″
D shelf 18⅝″ X 22⅝″
B shelf 18⅝″ X 34¾″
D side 18″ X 18¾″
D side 18″ X 18¾″
C top 23¾″ X 18¾″
C bottom 23¾″ X 18¾″
⅝″ MDO
C extra shelf (optional) 18⅝″ X 34¾″
E top 13¾″ X 27¼″
E bottom 13¾″ X 27¼″
E drawer fronts 4½″ X 13⅝″
E side 18″ X 27¼″
E side 18″ X 27¼″
F desk top 34″ X 32¼″
⅝″ MDO
Face grain
PLYWOOD LAYOUT
¼″ B-B
B back 36″ X 32″

35 5/16″
32¼″
34″
17¼″
1 X 4 (34″ long)
29″
34″ 1 X 4 front rail (back rail is 32½″ 1 X 4)
30¾″ 1 X 4
Hooks and eyes
29⅜″ 2 X 2
28⅜″ 2 X 2
Hinges
UNIT F
29⅜″
¼″ bevel both legs
Hook and eye
Countersink 2″ flathead screws

UNIT F. Fasten bottom of desk top section to folding desk top with piano hinge and finish the unit as explained above.

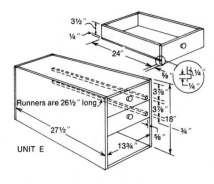

3½″
¼″
24″
⅝″
¼″
¼″
Runners are 26½″ long
3⅞″
3⅞″
18″
¾″
27½″
⅝″
13¾″
UNIT E

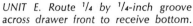

UNIT E. Route ¼ by ¼-inch groove across drawer front to receive bottom.

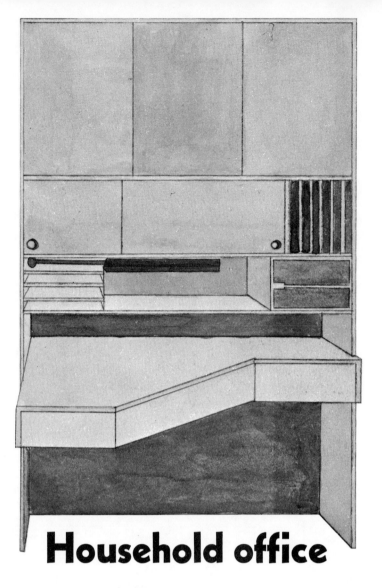

Household office

Here is a complete household office that only takes up 5½ feet of wall space. A platform-drawer, for a portable typewriter, that can be pushed into the desk is probably the most unusual feature. The front of the drawer is hinged so that it can drop down out of the way of the carriage. In order to provide support, the drawer extends back into the full depth of the desk.

A second drawer for supplies is at the opposite side of the desk, and directly above the desk's work surface are horizontal pigeonholes and sliding trays for important papers and desk paraphernalia. Above the open storage section, vertical files are kept on a shelf closed off by sliding hardboard doors. A showcase-type light fixture is mounted on a pivot so that it may be swung out and over the extended typewriter.

Basic material for the desk is ¾-inch plywood. A 4 by ⅛-inch iron plate is also required at the side of the typewriter drawer to steady the cantilevered corner and to counterbalance the weight of the machine.

Design: J. R. Davidson.

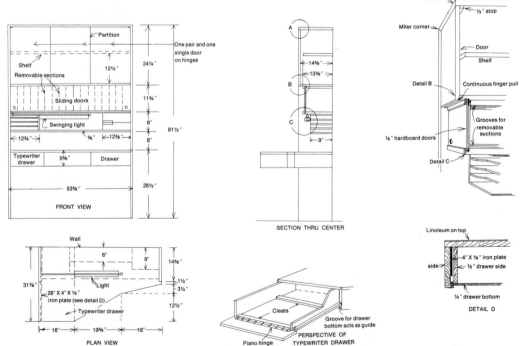

Business desk

Designed for a family room where two often work together, this work center offers generous knee space and a wide top. The design allows 47³/₄ inches between the drawers and the filing cabinet; the top (which can be covered with vinyl plastic) measures 82 by 34¹/₂ inches.

The desk plan helps keep the working surface clutter-free: a telephone hangs underneath in the knee space and a simple shelf across the top provides space for a clock, an adjustable lamp, and other items.

The 1 by 2 lumber at the top, front, and sides is rabbeted to hold the ³/₄-inch plywood supporting the top; corners are mitered. A second-hand steel filing cabinet is incorporated into the desk along with two smaller drawers (see page 91 for drawer construction). You may prefer to dispense with the filing cabinet and build both sides of the desk the same. The plywood shelf is supported with standard shelving brackets.

Design: Carl F. Gould.

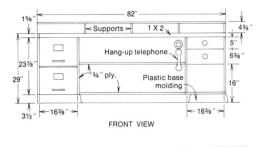

FRONT VIEW

TOP VIEW

DRAWER SECTION

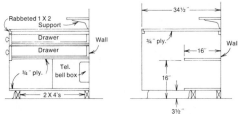

CENTER SECTION

Heavy-duty teak desk

This oversized desk with storage unit is a handsome addition to either home or office. It's divided into three separate sections: shelf unit, desk top, and legs.

The shelf unit rests on the desk top's side-rails, and small runners under the shelf unit keep it straight. Since it's not fastened in any way, it's easy to remove when you need an unobstructed working surface. If you prefer a lighter appearance, make the shelf unit smaller or substitute an open back.

The desk top includes three large drawers that are simple boxes with 1/4-inch plywood bottoms. If you extend the sides of each drawer a few inches beyond its rear wall, the drawer will not drop when pulled out. Thumb tacks under the drawers act as glides. Addition of some silicone lubricant at points of friction will help insure easy sliding.

The desk bottom and partitions are 1/2-inch shop-grade plywood. The trestle legs unscrew from the desk

top to make storage easy.

The desk shown was relatively expensive to build because most parts (legs, storage unit shelves, trim, surfaces) were made from teak and two 4 by 8-foot sheets of teak-veneered plywood. However, either mahogany or straight-grained fir would be a good alternative and could cut the cost in half.

You will need a radial arm saw (with dado attachment) and a 1/4-inch electric drill with an insetting bit and matching plug-cutter. The joinery is quite simple. Plywood edges are capped with 3/4-inch teak pieces (see illustration). This not only simplifies the joints but adds a distinctive border to all edges and corners.

Assemble with glue and 1-inch number 8 screws. The screws are inset and then covered with teak plugs.

Drawers and doors have a 3/4-inch overhang to eliminate pulls. A light oil finish completes the desk.

Design: Rick Morrall.

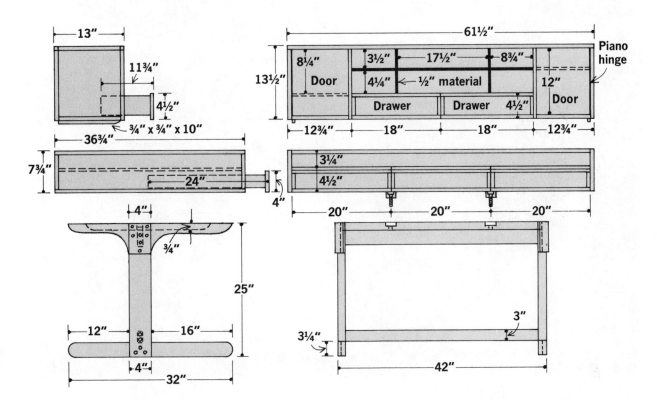

DESK boasts a full 36 by 60-inch surface, five drawers, two divided cupboards, and seven storage nooks. Four ¼-inch carriage bolts with wing nuts secure desk top to pedestal base.

TOP AND BOTTOM of desk are partitioned and joined with dividers glued in dado grooves.

SOLID TEAK EDGING, screwed and plugged, makes strong, attractive corners and borders that hide plywood edges.

A music center 8 feet long

This music center is designed in bold scale—it's large enough to house two speakers, turntable, amplifier, and radio tuner, with room to spare for storing records and tapes. Its teak finish and caned doors give it a rich, luxurious appearance.

Though the design is simple in concept, you should have reasonable proficiency in working with power tools before trying this piece. The materials are expensive and the degree of craftsmanship required is high.

Top, bottom, and sides are all cut from ³/₄-inch teak-veneered plywood with edges faced. The finish side of the plywood naturally faces out on the two sides, and up on the top and bottom. The back is cut from ¹/₄-inch teak wall paneling, finish side forward. The three vertical partitions and all shelves can be cut from any type of ³/₄-inch plywood (stain with teak finish, and face front edge with solid teak strip). Doors are simple frames of solid teak, joined in dowel-miter fashion (see page 89). Legs are the solid variety which come from the manufacturer with simple screw-in metal plates. A fifth leg is attached under the center of this unit for additional support, and the length to which all legs are cut allows vacuum cleaner access beneath the cabinet.

Cabinet corners are made from solid teak—turned at a 3¹/₈-inch diameter, bored out on the ends to allow insetting of cabinet face and back, and quartered (see illustration). Scrap pieces from the teak plywood are faced to form the abutting surfaces for doors. Before joining doors together, cut a groove wide enough to allow for inserting the caning spline.

To find machine-woven caning, look in the yellow pages of the phone book under "Chair Caning". Soak the caning in near-boiling water for several minutes. When thoroughly pliable, remove it from the water and center it on the frame. Be sure it extends ¹/₂-inch beyond the spline groove. Drive the webbing into the groove on one side with a mallet and hardwood wedge; repeat at the opposite side, then wedge it into top and bottom ends. Set the cutting edge of a chisel against the cane at the bottom outer corner of the groove, and strike the chisel-butt with a mallet just hard enough to cut the cane. Continue all along groove.

Squeeze some glue along groove, miter splines to fit, and drive them into place with a mallet and wooden wedge.

Design: William C. Sedlacek.

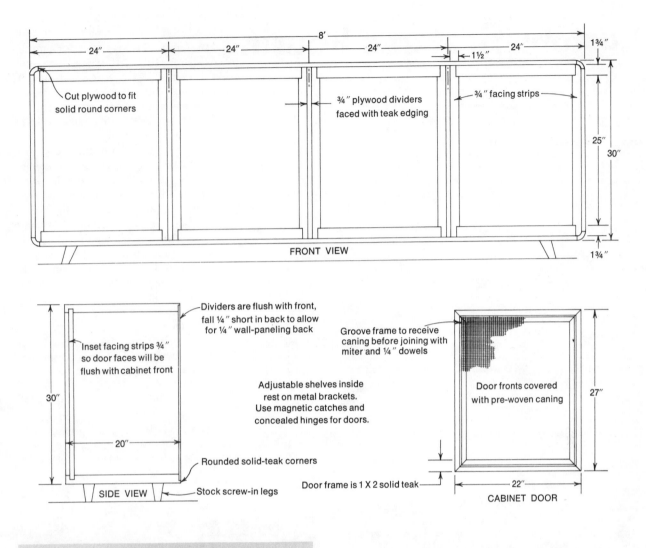

Cut plywood to fit solid round corners

¾" plywood dividers faced with teak edging

¾" facing strips

24" · 24" · 24" · 24"

8'

1¾"

25"

30"

1½"

1¾"

FRONT VIEW

Dividers are flush with front, fall ¼" short in back to allow for ¼" wall-paneling back

Inset facing strips ¾" so door faces will be flush with cabinet front

30"

20"

SIDE VIEW

Rounded solid-teak corners

Stock screw-in legs

Adjustable shelves inside rest on metal brackets. Use magnetic catches and concealed hinges for doors.

Groove frame to receive caning before joining with miter and ¼" dowels

Door fronts covered with pre-woven caning

27"

Door frame is 1 X 2 solid teak

22"

CABINET DOOR

CORNERS are made from solid teak, turned to 3¹⁄₈-inch diameter, bored out, and quartered (see sketch at right).

FIRST POUND CANE in groove with wooden wedge; cut along bottom corner and glue; and drive spline in place.

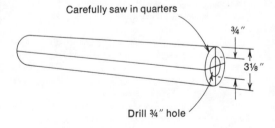

Carefully saw in quarters

¾"

3⅛"

Drill ¾" hole

SOLID CORNER PIECE

Custom-fit stereo housing

A good-looking cabinet built to fit a stereo system is a must for a music-loving family. The handsome unit shown is 47½ inches high and 91 inches wide, but you can vary dimensions to fit your equipment.

Make the basic framework by notching the six front and back horizontal 2 by 4's to fit the eight vertical 2 by 2's. Set five 2 by 2's between each pair of 2 by 4's and mark for holes through all members, including vertical 2 by 2's and the partial back of ⅝-inch plywood. Bolt frame together with ¼-inch threaded rods.

One-half-inch plywood panels are glued and nailed (use finishing nails) to both sides of the vertical 2 by 2's, inset from front ½-inch. These make the "walls" of the cabinet. Provide 3½-inch toe space by setting the unit on a frame of 2 by 4's. The ¾-inch plywood doors shown are optional for middle and lower center sections. For ¼-inch plywood record album dividers, rout ¼-inch-wide grooves on 4-inch centers across top center section. Speaker areas should be covered with fabric.

Design: Donald Wm. MacDonald, AIA.

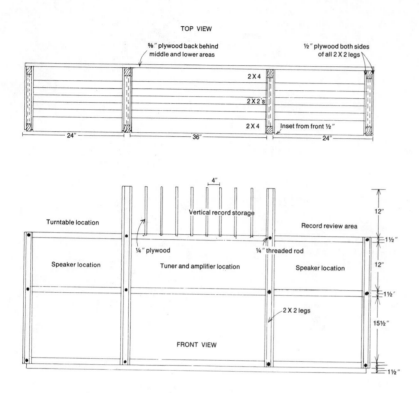

TOP VIEW

⅝″ plywood back behind middle and lower areas

½″ plywood both sides of all 2 X 2 legs

2 X 4

2 X 2's

2 X 4

Inset from front ½″

24″ 36″ 24″

4″

Vertical record storage

Turntable location

¼″ plywood

¼″ threaded rod

Record review area

12″

1½″

Speaker location

Tuner and amplifier location

Speaker location

12″

1½″

2 X 2 legs

15½″

FRONT VIEW

1½″

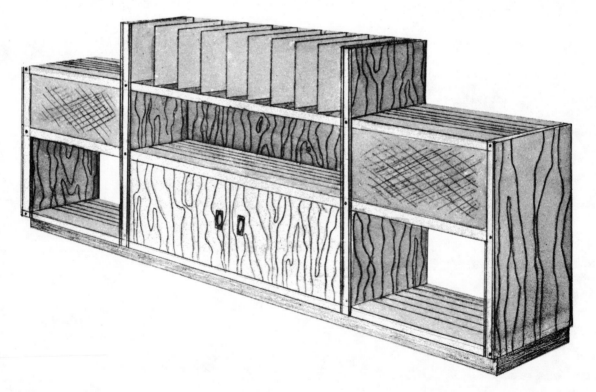

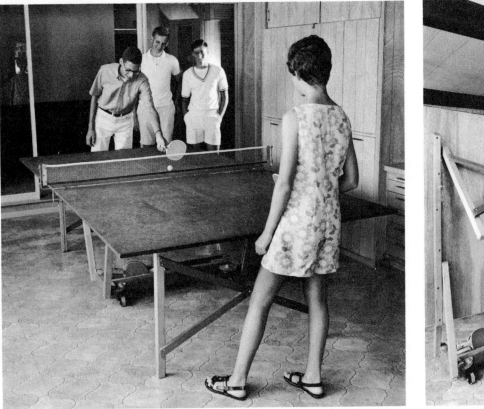

Folding, rolling ping-pong table

Level and solid enough to satisfy even expert players, this ping-pong table nevertheless folds up quickly for storage. It is inexpensive to build; main cost is the 5 by 9-foot, ⅝-inch-thick plywood regulation top.

This top, cut in half and then connected with a piano hinge, folds as shown above. The two folded halves are held together for storage by one small C-clamp; the end legs simply fold down against the plywood top sections.

As shown in the drawing, there are 1-inch-thick wood stops on the underside of the plywood top and on the shelf base. These stops keep the two halves of the top vertical when folded and clamped. Cut the stops to fit and attach them *after* the rest of the table is assembled.

Finish the top with the dull green paint made for ping-pong tables.

CENTRAL SUPPORT is sturdy; provides shelf for storing equipment.

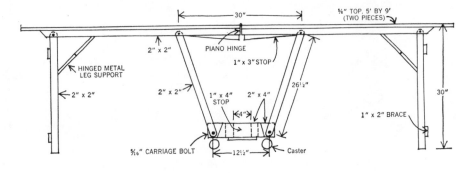

Lamp bases

Lamps are both functional and fun to make. The main work lies in creating the base—electrical parts and shades are inexpensive and best purchased ready-made. Although the simple bases on these two pages are of wood, don't limit your materials. Look around the house and see what's available—ceramic objects, acrylic plastic, bottles, metal, even concrete. Once you've selected a material, check on the types of available electrical fixtures and purchase the one that's easiest to attach to your base.

Two 1 by 12-inch boards—with a circle and a long $^3/_4$-inch-wide notch cut in each—can be slipped together to form an interesting floor lamp (see right). The circle is to accommodate the round globe. As shown, the lamp can be used either with or without its top, or the top can be turned upside-down to hold the globe as a desk lamp.

The floor lamp pictured is 5 feet tall (with the top on). Center of the 8-inch-diameter circle cut-out is 12 inches from one end. Before cutting the circle, mark the center, draw a line across the width of the board through the mark, and cut the end off. Then use a coping or keyhole saw to cut a half-circle out of each piece. The cord is hidden behind a strip of corner molding glued to one of the boards. If you wish, you can dowel the top to the base (without glue). The lamp is easily demountable for moving.

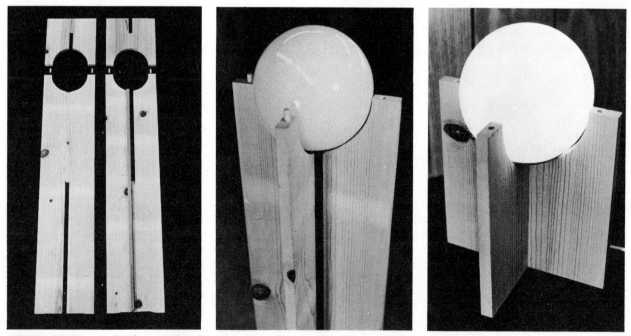

PIECES NEEDED to make the complete floor lamp are shown at left. The top is doweled to the base without glue. The lamp can be used without the top, or the top can be turned upside down and used as a desk lamp.

Mushroom-shaped lamp is easily made by mounting a light fixture in an imported wood canister, then setting an antique frosted globe on top. Instead of the antique globe, you can use a regular round one—or try the ornate type often used in hall ceiling fixtures. A wooden canister like this one can be purchased in almost any import shop—choose one of the right scale and dimension to suit the globe you decide to use. For the light fixture, you will need 8 feet of cord, one electric plug, a cord switch, a porcelain light socket, a plastic bushing, and a 40-watt light bulb. A block of wood is glued onto the bottom of the canister to raise the socket and bulb into the globe for better illumination.

Let your imagination go. Some very attractive lamp bases can be made of scrap wood from the bottom of your wood pile. If you have a drill bit long enough (for the cord hole), you can use a large chunk of wood—such as a piece of railroad tie or a cylindrical length of redwood. If you lack such a long drill bit, then bore through smaller single blocks and laminate them together with glue and clamps. Different types and colors of wood can be particularly handsome when they are laminated together.

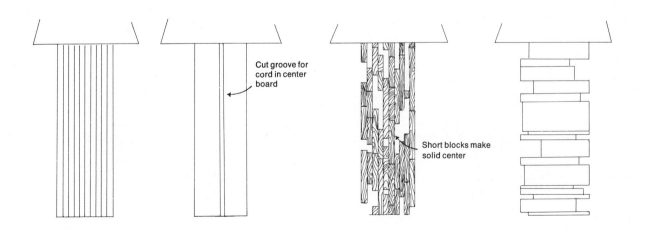

Cut groove for cord in center board

Short blocks make solid center

Lamps with built-on shades

Making a lamp—shade and all—allows the ultimate in creativity. Suggested here are two well-designed lamps with shades that you can make. Shades can be fashioned from wrapped cord or twine; you can stretch fabric across the wooden frame, or attach acrylic sheet plastic with screws (see tips on working with this material, page 86). The bases are wood.

Design: Donald Wm. MacDonald, AIA.

Short in size and simple to make, this lamp has framing of 1 by 1-inch wood and a base of 10-inch-high 8 by 8-inch kiln-dried lumber. A $^1/_4$-inch hole is drilled up through the base for the cord and a groove is cut across the bottom, allowing the base to sit flat over the cord. Lap joints are used at the corners between horizontal members. Secure with glue and screws. This project takes a standard lamp fixture.

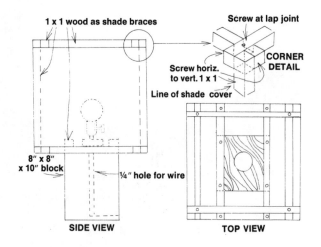

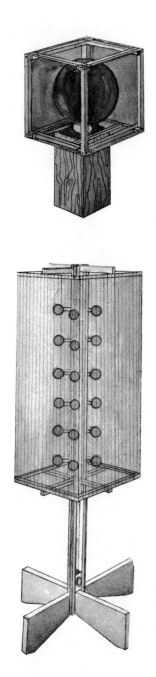

Sixteen small light bulbs help give this lamp a distinctive modern character. Small no-switch lamp holders (available in hardware and lighting stores) are attached diagonally to the four 1 by 1 center pieces with hollow threaded rods. Most of the framing is of 1 by 1-inch stock, but the top-piece is a 1 by 3 and base is cut from 1 by 6. Shade frame-corners are lap-joined; all other corners are butt-joined (see page 89). Use glue and screws. A rheostat can be added to the lamp base for brightness control. Try 15-watt bulbs.

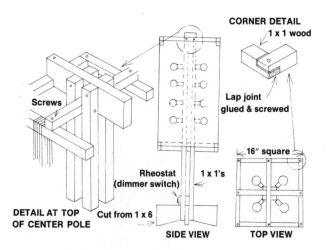

Two lampshades

Lampshades can be fun as well as functional. Here are two styles that do the job, are good looking, inexpensive, and easy to make. Both are made to fit ceiling-type fixtures, but with a little imagination may be converted to fit table or floor lamps.

Tiffany-style lampshade is made with an ivy-training frame, half a yard of bright 45-inch fabric, a spray-can of flat black paint, and upholstery thread.

First select the frame (several sizes are available at nursery supply stores). Cut an opening at the top with wire-cutters for your light fixture and spray the frame with paint. To measure for the fabric cover, figure the length as circumference of the frame plus 1 inch (for seam), and the width as the distance from center-top of frame to bottom edge plus 3 inches (for hems and turn at the base of the frame). The fabric on the lamp shown was 13 by 45 inches before sewing (circumference is 44 inches).

With the outer sides together, stitch crosswise seam; then stitch 1-inch hems along both long edges to form casing, leaving small openings to insert the drawstring. Turn right side out.

Using a strong thread, gather top to a small circle about 3½ inches in diameter and tie tightly. Pull the fabric over the frame, position and gather with thread, then tie. Trim the thread ends, and it's ready to hang.

Tulip shade is easily made by attaching loosely woven material for "petals" over a frame of reed splines (obtainable from suppliers of chair caning). Soak splines until pliable; cut to length and bevel ends as needed; then fasten together with pins (a beach ball protected with cardboard makes a good mold). Let dry, then glue joints as shown. Cut petals (those in the picture are abaca cloth), glue, and pin until set. Cut opening in top to fit over fixture when globe is removed. Secure shade with tape if needed. The lamp may be either painted or stained.

START with painted frame and fabric. Gather hemmed edge tightly with heavy upholstery thread.

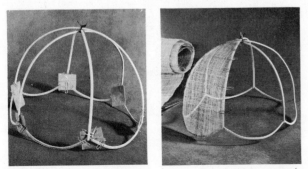

SECURE CROSSED SPLINES at top with wire; hold framework with paper clips and cardboard until glue dries. Cut cloth petals from paper pattern; hold with paper clips or glue.

Headboards with cabinets

Here are a couple of headboards that are handsome as well as utilitarian. Both feature cabinet-tables on each side for telephone, clock, radio, and books. Telephone book and other articles are stored beneath.

Central wood sections can be built to fit a double, queen, or king-sized bed. Both headboards are attached to the wall with metal brackets, purchased at a hardware store. They can be moved by simply unscrewing the brackets.

This headboard is made from ¾-inch hardwood-veneered plywood, faced around edges with matching solid 1 by 2. Two sections within the plywood panel are cut out and mounted on piano hinges — these may be propped open with small hinged braces to serve as back rests. Bedside stands, bolted to headboard, are ¾-inch plywood boxes with tops of hardwood plywood. Switches control reading light.

Design: James Jennings, AIA.

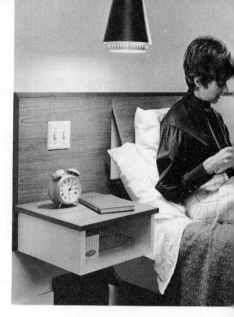

Stained ash boards give this headboard a rich appearance. Tabletops at each side and the full-length top shelf are surfaced with laminated plastic (see page 87). Side tables are of ¾-inch plywood—edges are surfaced with ash trim. Underneath each tabletop is a simple box of ¼-inch plywood, painted black, for storage.

The headboard is secured (with flush metal mounts) to a 1 by 3 on the wall. Correct spacing at the bottom is maintained by adding small wood blocks.

Design: Richard R. Griffiths, AIA.

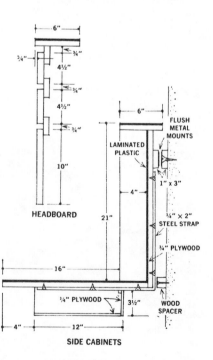

Bed and wall shelving unit

You can provide key room decor with a bed and shelving headboard arrangement like this. The shelving unit is quickly and easily constructed from kiln-dried 2 by 12 lumber. Shelves are dadoed into vertical boards, glued, and nailed. The bed is made by laying 1⅛-inch plywood (purchased at a major lumberyard) on a rectangular frame of mitered 2 by 12's. Size of the bed is determined by your mattress size. No springs are used. Edge-facing for the plywood is 1 by 2-inch stock, mitered at end corners and butted into shelves. Fabric to match the bedspread is mounted on the wall in the headboard area. For reading, you can add a light fixture to the underside of the shelving that extends over the head of the bed. Shelving can be nailed to the wall through the sides.

Design: Donald Wm. MacDonald, AIA.

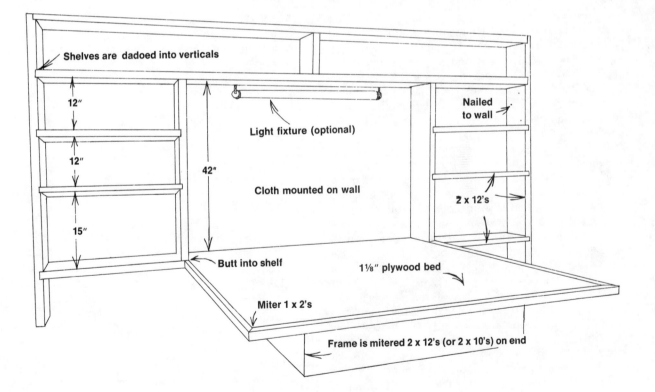

Shelves are dadoed into verticals

12"

12"

15"

42"

Light fixture (optional)

Cloth mounted on wall

Nailed to wall

2 x 12's

Butt into shelf

1⅛" plywood bed

Miter 1 x 2's

Frame is mitered 2 x 12's (or 2 x 10's) on end

Captain's bed sleeps two

This fold-up captain's bed is ideal for turning a spare room into a bedroom to accommodate overnight guests. It's great for lounging at any time, but when guests stay over, it quickly and easily pulls out into a king-sized bed. Three large drawers in the base store blankets and sheets, and the long storage compartment above the drawers holds a second polyurethane foam mattress (to be added next to the one on top when the bed is pulled out).

This convertible bed is made primarily from plywood. The one shown has sides and front constructed of $3/4$-inch mahogany solid-core plywood, but a less expensive version could be made from $3/4$-inch fir plywood, stained or painted. The bed measures $6^1/2$ feet long, $3^1/2$ feet wide, and 2 feet high when closed. Pulled out, it is a full $6^1/2$ feet wide. No springs are required; foam mattresses are supported by $5/8$-inch plywood. Shelf for the spare mattress is $1/2$-inch plywood and the back is cut from $1/4$-inch plywood.

The ends of the bed provide all necessary support. Framing members are anchored to the inside of the end-panels with glue and screws. Card-table braces allow the solid $2^1/2$ by $2^1/2$-inch legs to swing down and lock into place. The long storage door is attached to the $1/2$-inch plywood with a 6-foot piano hinge (centered 3 inches in from each end). Each of the two center drawer dividers is made from a $5/8$-inch plywood scrap, glued and nailed between two 2 by 3's. Drawers are carefully cut to fit the two outer 2 by 3 "runners."

All exposed plywood edges are faced with strips of solid mahogany. The bed pictured was finished with a clear polyurethane finish.

Design: Donald W. Vandervort.

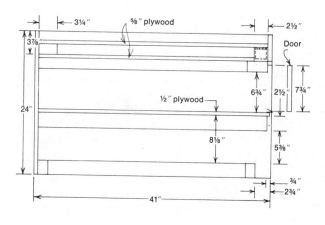

END VIEW (CLOSED)

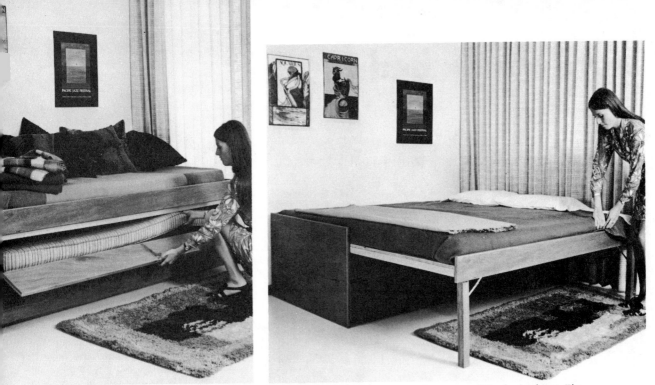

SPARE POLYURETHANE FOAM MATTRESS is stored in the long compartment at the center of the bed cabinet. The top section slides out and drops into place to make a king-sized bed.

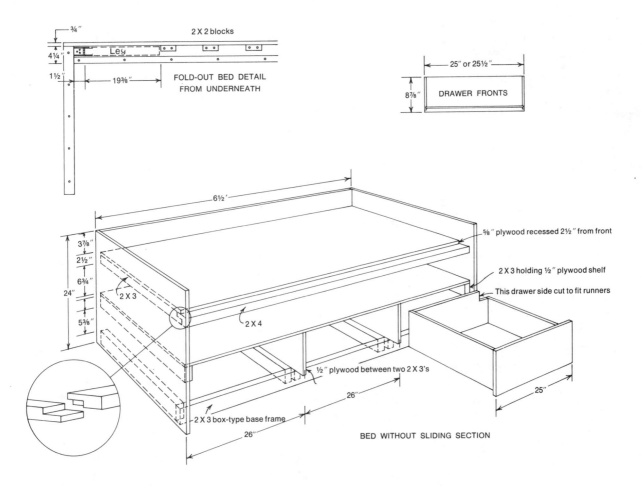

¾"

2 X 2 blocks

4¼"

Leg

1½"

19⅜"

FOLD-OUT BED DETAIL
FROM UNDERNEATH

25" or 25½"

8⅞"

DRAWER FRONTS

6½'

⅝" plywood recessed 2½" from front

2 X 3 holding ½" plywood shelf

This drawer side cut to fit runners

3⅞"
2½"
6¾"
24"
5⅜"

2 X 3

2 X 4

½" plywood between two 2 X 3's

25"

26"

2 X 3 box-type base frame

26"

BED WITHOUT SLIDING SECTION

Sturdy bunk bed

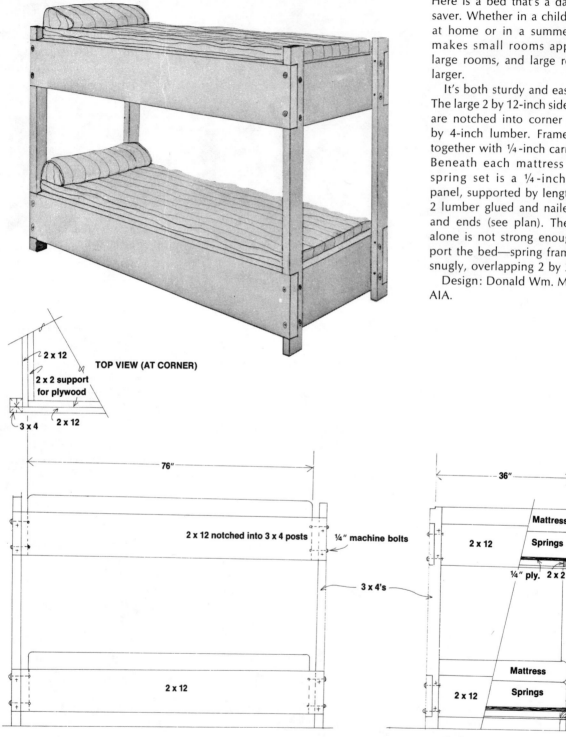

Here is a bed that's a dandy space-saver. Whether in a children's room at home or in a summer cabin, it makes small rooms appear to be large rooms, and large rooms even larger.

It's both sturdy and easy to build. The large 2 by 12-inch sides and ends are notched into corner posts of 3 by 4-inch lumber. Frame is bolted together with ¼-inch carriage bolts. Beneath each mattress and bedspring set is a ¼-inch plywood panel, supported by lengths of 2 by 2 lumber glued and nailed to sides and ends (see plan). The plywood alone is not strong enough to support the bed—spring frame must fit snugly, overlapping 2 by 2's.

Design: Donald Wm. MacDonald, AIA.

2 x 12

2 x 2 support for plywood

TOP VIEW (AT CORNER)

3 x 4

2 x 12

76"

2 x 12 notched into 3 x 4 posts

¼" machine bolts

3 x 4's

2 x 12

SIDE VIEW

36"

Mattress

4"

2 x 12

Springs

1½"

¼" ply. 2 x 2

42"

Mattress

1½"

2 x 12

Springs

20"

4"

END VIEW

SECTION

"Campaign" chest

Here is a chest of drawers that is easily made with the help of a table saw or radial-arm saw. If you don't have one of these tools, you can revise the design and make the piece with hand tools. The dimensions of the chest shown are intended to keep material costs to a minimum.

The top, sides, and front are made from ¾-inch plywood—use one 4 by 8-foot hardboard-veneered, or fir panel. Also required are one 4 by 4-foot panel of ¾-inch A-D fir for drawer sides and backs, and a full sheet of ¼-inch plywood for drawer bottoms and the cabinet back. Two 24½-inch lengths of 2 by 4, located at the bottom of the chest, hold sides in place.

Top of the cabinet is mitered to sides, glued, and nailed with small finishing nails. For additional strength, attach sides to undersurface of top with metal corner brackets. Back is rabbeted into top and sides. Drawer runners are glued and nailed into place. When cutting side panels, account for ¼-inch edge facing on plywood. Below the bottom drawer, a 2-inch-wide piece of matching ¾-inch plywood extends to the floor (nailed to the front of the 2 by 4).

A power saw with dado-blade assembly is needed to make the type of drawer shown. If you have a power saw but lack a dado assembly, make two cuts with a standard blade (set ½-inch high) across drawer sides and front to make a ¼-inch groove for bottom to fit in; rabbet front and use butt joint for drawer back. Drawer slides on *top* of runners. Add a runner to the front of the cabinet (extend drawer front down low enough to hide this front runner). If you have no power saw, glue and nail drawer bottom flush to bottom of sides and back.

For dado-cut drawer runners, you will need about 20 feet of ½ by ¾-inch stock. Otherwise, about 33 feet of 1 by ¾-inch stock will be needed for front and side runners.

"Campaign chest" corner fixtures and handles, purchased at a builder's supply store, can be added for decoration.

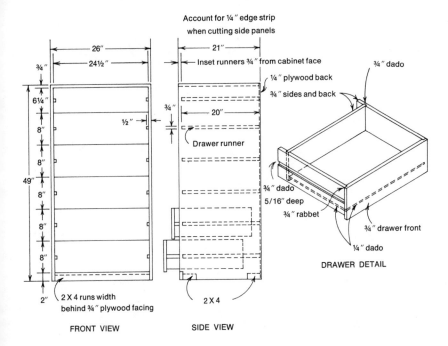

FRONT VIEW   SIDE VIEW   DRAWER DETAIL

Dowels make a wine rack

Two sizes of dowels, some white glue, and an electric drill are all you need to make this wooden wine rack. The one shown holds nine bottles—you can make yours bigger or smaller, as you prefer.

Buy about 12 feet each of ³⁄₈ and 1¹⁄₄-inch doweling. Cut the ³⁄₈-inch size into 16 pieces 3⁵⁄₈ inches long and 6 pieces 12 inches long. Cut the ¹⁄₄-inch doweling into 12 pieces 11 inches long. Lightly sand all parts.

Make the three horizontal levels first. For each level, drill holes (using a ³⁄₈-inch spade bit) halfway through the ends of two of the 11-inch dowels and all the way through the other two. (To avoid breakout problems, drill from one side until the bit point protrudes; then turn and complete the hole from the opposite side.) Insert two 12-inch dowels and glue tightly. Check to make sure that all three levels are identical in size and shape.

Drill ¹⁄₂-inch-deep holes for the vertical dowels into both sides of one unit, and one side of each of the other two.

Begin final assembly, using glue and patience to insure rigidity. Insert eight dowels into the bottom unit and press the middle level over these. With a steel square, check for right angles. Let glue dry. Insert remaining dowels into middle unit, press top unit over, and check again for right angles. For a finish, apply Danish oil.

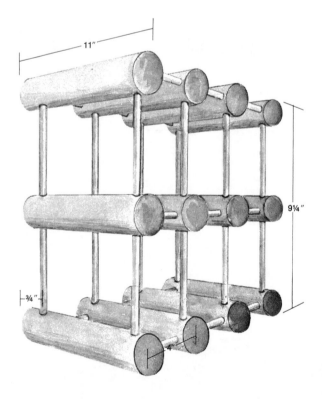

Spanish-style wine storage

Here is a wine rack that you can build to suit almost any family-sized wine cache. Made from 6-inch hollow clay tiles (the eight-sided variety) housed between sections of 3 by 12-inch kiln-dried lumber, it's an attractive, sturdy piece of furniture.

Decide upon the number of tiles you wish to have; they will be stacked 3 tiles high. The number is up to you but if you plan a rack exceeding 10 tiles in length, it is best to build a second unit.

Construction is simple. Dado a ¾-inch-deep by 2½-inch-wide groove 14 inches in from each end (on one side) of both vertical boards. Secure horizontal members in the dado grooves with glue and lag bolts.

Design: Donald Wm. MacDonald, AIA.

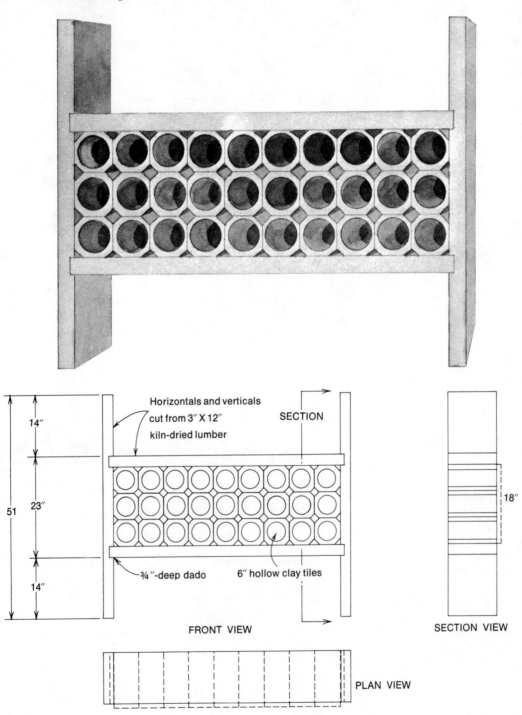

Horizontals and verticals cut from 3" X 12" kiln-dried lumber

SECTION

14"

51

23"

14"

¾"-deep dado

6" hollow clay tiles

FRONT VIEW

18"

SECTION VIEW

PLAN VIEW

Kitchen cart with swing-up leaves

Large enough to be of real use when serving company, this cart is neatly "garaged" in a kitchen base cabinet. When rolled out and its two drop-leaf ends raised, it is almost 6 feet long. It can serve as a buffet as well as a cart for clearing dishes from the dining room table.

This 20-inch-wide cart is made of walnut and walnut plywood. Each drop-leaf end is supported, when up, by one sliding wood piece. A pair of casters carry one end; two fixed rollers at the other end make the cart easy to steer. The top and both drop-leaves have walnut edgings that extend a full inch above the top level to keep dishes from sliding off when the cart is moved.

Design: Richard Perkins, AIA.

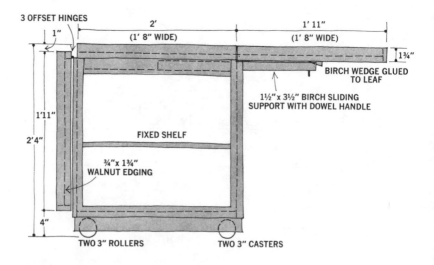

3 OFFSET HINGES

1"

2' (1' 8" WIDE)

1' 11" (1' 8" WIDE)

1¾"

BIRCH WEDGE GLUED TO LEAF

1½" x 3½" BIRCH SLIDING SUPPORT WITH DOWEL HANDLE

1'11"

2'4"

FIXED SHELF

¾" x 1¾" WALNUT EDGING

4"

TWO 3" ROLLERS

TWO 3" CASTERS

Home bar...made with wall paneling

Delightful for entertaining, this bar is good looking, inexpensive, and relatively easy to make. Plenty of counter space, shelves for storing glasses and bottles, and a pull-out ice container make mixing and serving a pleasure for the host.

Walnut wall paneling on the front, sides, and part of the back gives this bar a handsome appearance at small cost—and no finish is required. The counter top is made from plastic laminate laid on a ¾-inch plywood base (for directions on working with plastic laminate, see page 87). A ¾-inch aluminum edging circles the top.

Behind the bar, two sliding doors of textured plastic sheet help keep out dust but allow quick access to glasses. Below, ¼-inch hardboard doors slide open to reveal further storage and a pullout ice bin (a section of ¾-inch plywood is cut to hold a small plastic wastebasket). Paneling or plastic sheet may be used for these sliding doors.

Design: Albert C. Lechner.

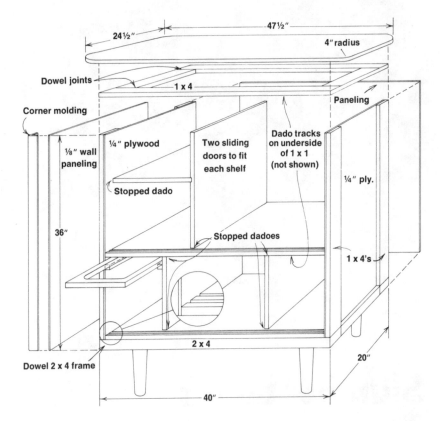

Here are a couple of sturdy, inexpensive children's beds with built-in room decor. They are lightweight, demountable, and you can arrange them in any of several ways: side-by-side, face-to-face, or L-shape. The inside of each frame measures 3 feet 3 inches wide by 6 feet 4 inches long (accommodating a standard twin-sized mattress). Optional storage boxes serve as bedroom stools.

The bed shown was made from five 4 by 8-foot sheets of ³/₄-inch DFPA-grade plywood, (Medium Density Overlay plywood provides an ideal surface for painting). You will also need forty 2-inch metal corner brackets for fastening pieces together, 2 boxes of #6 by ³/₄-inch flathead screws for attaching corner brackets, twenty-eight #8 by 1¹/₄-inch screws for runners, and twelve plated #8 by 1¹/₂-inch ovalhead screws for fastening canopy to bed.

For storage boxes, you will need an extra panel of ¹/₂-inch plywood and one pound of 6d finishing nails for bottoms, sides, and supports (countersink and fill nailholes). You may want four 1⁷/₈-inch by 2¹/₂-inch flush ring-pulls for handles.

It's best to undercoat all plywood

Slumber bunks

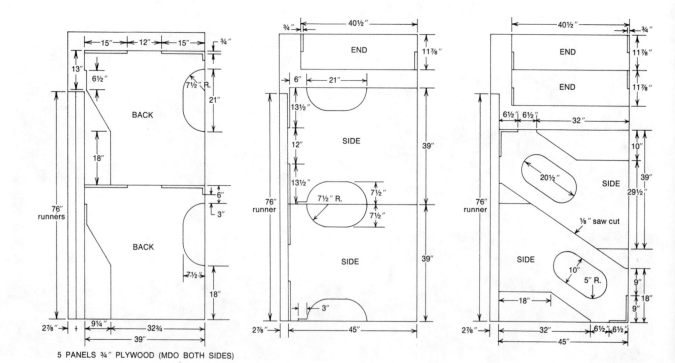

5 PANELS ¾" PLYWOOD (MDO BOTH SIDES)

parts *before* beginning construction. Also, read "Working with Plywood", page 84.

After cutting out all pieces, determine how low runners should be for bedsprings, then screw them in place (pre-drill and countersink screw holes). If you don't have bedsprings, use a panel of ½-inch fir plywood, adding runners at head and foot of bed. Fasten bed sides and ends with corner brackets. Assemble canopy with brackets and attach it to the bed (two screws through back and each side).

Boxes are glued and nailed to-gether (see illustration at right). Set inner support panels ¼-inch below top of box. For lifting the lid, either chisel a hole for a flush ring-pull, drill a 1-inch finger hole in top, or cut a half-circle at top of a side panel. Decals or self-sticking letters can be added after painting.

Plywood edges should be sanded, filled with surfacing putty, and sealed before painting. Paint with high-grade interior type enamel. Use masking tape to insure straight paint lines.

Design: Arvid Orbeck.

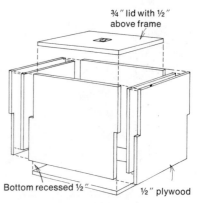

¾" lid with ½" above frame

Bottom recessed ½"   ½" plywood

BOX ASSEMBLY

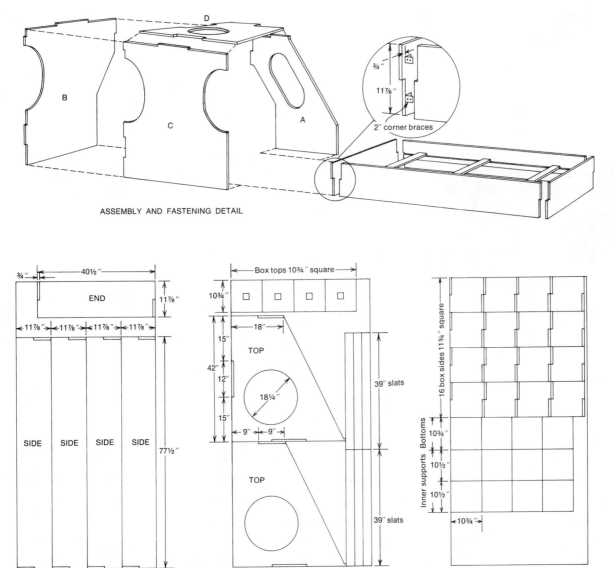

ASSEMBLY AND FASTENING DETAIL

3/4"

11⅞"

2" corner braces

END — 40½" — ¾" — 11⅞"

11⅞" 11⅞" 11⅞" 11⅞"

SIDE   SIDE   SIDE   SIDE   77½"

Box tops 10¾" square

10¾"

18"

15"

TOP

42"   18¼"

12"

15"

9" 9"

TOP

13½" 12" 13½"
39"

39" slats

39" slats

16 box sides 11¾" square

Inner supports Bottoms

10¾"

10½"

10½"

10¾"

1 PANEL ½" PLYWOOD (MDO BOTH SIDES)

Child-sized lounge with toy hideaway

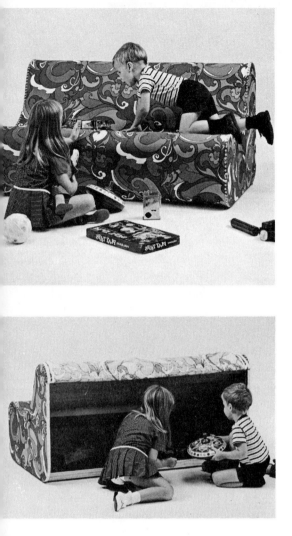

This delightful lounge is for children. It is scaled to their size and built for reading, resting, and romping. As the picture left shows, it is also a large storage chest for toys. Its wood framing is easy to build with only a few tools, and the upholstering (often a difficult job) is very simple. The basic design is so useful that you could also scale this lounge a bit larger so that everyone could use it—in a family room or, with a durable plastic-surfaced fabric, on a patio or deck.

To build it in the size shown, first cut the two ends out of $3/4$-inch plywood to approximately the shape shown in sketch (see "Working with Plywood", page 84). Then cut the two 2 by 2's and two 1 by $7\frac{1}{2}$-inch pieces of clear fir (or similar wood) to $52\frac{1}{2}$ inches and attach them to the plywood ends with white glue and screws. The 1 by $7\frac{1}{2}$-inch pieces should be a full 1 inch thick—*not* $3/4$ inch—to give strength (or use 2 by 8's which actually measure $1\frac{1}{2}$ by $7\frac{1}{2}$ inches).

Cut a toy shelf of $1/8$-inch hardboard or $1/4$-inch plywood to fit over and attach to the 2 by 2's; use white glue and small nails.

To upholster the lounge, you will need a 54-inch length of 8-inch cylindrical polyurethane foam, 10 feet of 30-inch-wide heavy upholsterer's burlap, and $3\frac{1}{2}$ yards of 60-inch-wide upholstery fabric (all obtainable at upholstery shops).

Have the shop cut the foam in half lengthwise—or do it yourself using a serrated bread knife—and rubber-cement the two halves to the 1 by $7\frac{1}{2}$-inch members, as shown. The foam will be slightly overlong—tuck the ends up to give extra padding on the ends of the lounge.

Cover the plywood ends with the upholstery fabric you have chosen, using tacks or a staple gun to affix it to the insides of the plywood ends.

Cut and sew the burlap to make a single piece that will cover the front, seat, seat back, and top (but not the open back). Overlap and double-stitch the seams for strength. Tack the burlap along the top edge of the back first, then tack it down the sides, stretching it as tight as you can and turning edges under. Keep the tacks on the inner edges of the plywood ends to leave room for ornamental upholstery tacks.

Sew hook-and-pile tape to the two sides of the section of decorative fabric that will hang down to enclose the back of the lounge and staple or tack the matching strip to the back edges of the plywood ends. Then stretch the upholstery fabric and tack on over the burlap, again turning edges under and using ornamental upholstery tacks about 1 inch apart on the ends of the lounge.

Design: Rick Morrall.

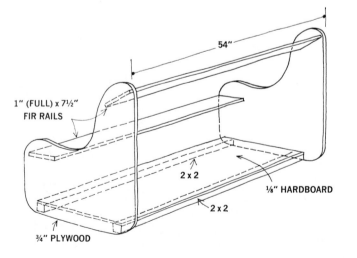

1" (FULL) x 7½" FIR RAILS
54"
2 x 2
⅛" HARDBOARD
2 x 2
¾" PLYWOOD

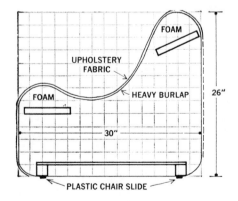

FOAM
UPHOLSTERY FABRIC
FOAM
HEAVY BURLAP
26"
30"
PLASTIC CHAIR SLIDE

The bed is the playhouse roof

Most children's rooms aren't big enough to accommodate a bed and a playhouse. This one has both in combination form.

The bed is actually a table with 2 by 4 legs, 2 by 3 frame, and ½-inch plywood top covered with a single-bed mattress. The playhouse is created by a hinged two-piece, ¾-inch plywood unit that fits around two sides of the table-bed. The entire space inside is for play. Three small arched doors open in; inside are assorted hooks, bolts, and latches for busy work. Finger holes function as handles and also make good peep holes.

A 5-inch-high railing around the top of the plywood unit keeps a young child from falling out of bed. Two toe-slits cut through the plywood sides make it easy to climb up and down.

The enclosure is painted white and the doors bright magenta; the decorative trim is magenta and orange. The sides measure 6 feet 3 inches, the ends 3 feet 4 inches. Four barrel bolts mounted on the inside of the plywood sides hold panels to the table-bed frame. However, there's no need to remove the enclosure for bed making or even for vacuuming inside the playhouse.

The playhouse is also useful as a storage place for games and toys that would ordinarily clutter up the floor. Doors could be enlarged to accommodate a trike or wagon.

Design: Rick Lambert.

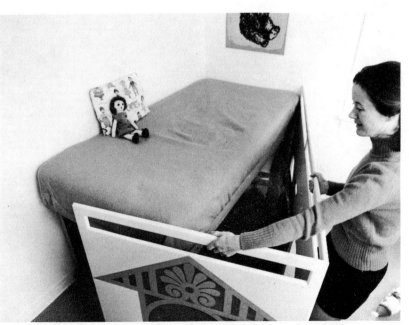

HINGED SIDES of the plywood enclosure fit around the bed. They are fastened to the bed with barrel bolts (to allow easy removal).

Worktable a child can grow with

Here is a child's worktable and storage unit that can change its height when the youngster is about to outgrow it. As illustrated above, the tabletop is 24³/₄ inches high—just right for the 6-year-old in the photograph.

In a few years, when the table gets too low, the whole unit can be turned upside down. This brings the working surface up to 28³/₄ inches, because the storage boxes originally on top are 4 inches higher than those on the bottom. When you turn it over, the tabletop—a hollow-core door faced on both sides with hardboard—is reversed as well, providing a clean, unmarked work top to use at the new height.

The unit can be built with hand tools if you use grooved plywood (see page 84) for the sides of the boxes and use the grooves to support the sliding shelves (as shown in the photograph, plastic dishpans will also slide in grooves). Otherwise, you will need a power saw with dado blades.

The unit is made of four plywood boxes, two base units, and the door. The base is attached with angle brackets and the boxes are screwed to the tabletop.

Insulation board is set between the boxes for a tack board and is moved to the upper side when the unit is turned over. (It will be higher than the back but is easily cut to fit.)

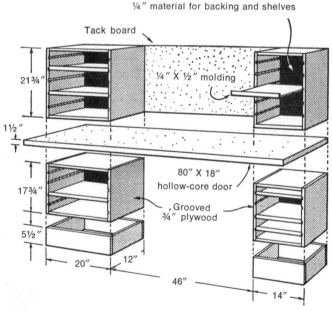

¼" material for backing and shelves

Tack board

¼" X ½" molding

21¾"

1½"

17¾"

80" X 18"
hollow-core door

Grooved
¾" plywood

5½"

20" 12"

46"

14"

EXPLODED VIEW

An oversized art table

Creativity will flourish on the open space of this art table. It provides an 8-foot-long surface where two or even three youngsters can spread out large newsprint pads and sheets of colored paper, and still have room to spare for craft materials.

It is made from a single sheet of plywood, edging strips, some scrap ¾-inch plywood, and a length of 2 by 4 lumber. The cost is slight, considering the six or more years a child can use it. The plywood top is coated with a clear sealer so that crayons, glue, and paint won't penetrate.

To make the art table, you'll need one 4 by 8-foot sheet of ¾-inch plywood, two 10-foot lengths and two 3-foot lengths of 1 by 2 trim, and one 6-foot 2 by 4. You'll also need two 8 by 24-inch scraps of ¾-inch plywood.

The top and all the leg pieces are cut from the single sheet of plywood as shown in the sketch (for techniques used in working with plywood, see page 84). Cut the tabletop 28 by 96 inches. Cut four leg-sides 15½ inches tall by 23½ inches wide to the outside miter. Cut four leg-ends 15½ inches tall by 3¾ inches wide to the outside miter.

From the scrap ¾-inch plywood, saw two pieces 8 by 24 inches to be used as leg attaching-plates. Cut the four 1 by 2 edging strips for the top: two of them 28 inches long and two 96 inches long—both to the inside miter.

With finishing nails and glue, attach edging strips to top and assemble the two hollow legs. Screw the plates to the legs as shown in sketch. Then screw the plates to the underside of the table, about 2 inches in from the ends and centered front to back. Glue and screw the 2 by 4 brace along the center, lengthwise under the table. Lightly sand all surfaces and finish with a clear sealer.

Design: Gordon Hammond.

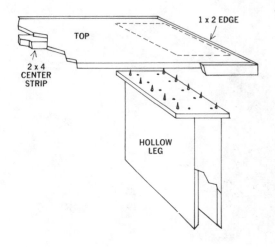

HOLLOW LEGS are recessed out of the way at table's ends. The 17-inch height is right for young children.

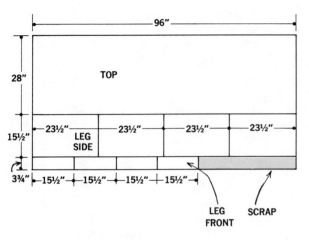

CUT PIECES from single sheet of plywood—cutting plan shown here is designed for economy.

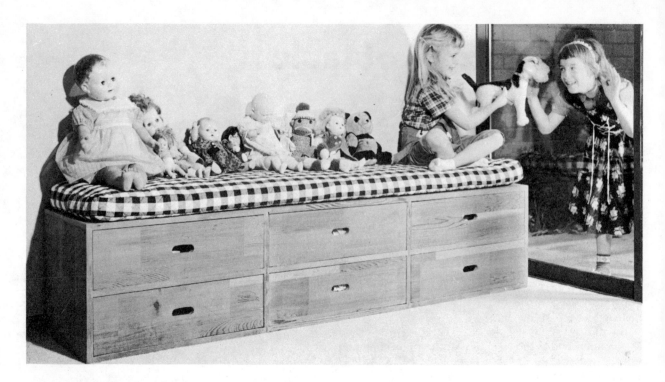

Play chest

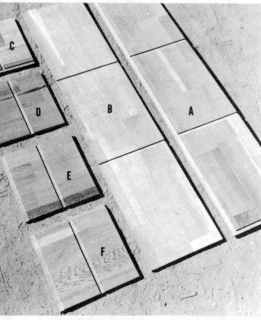

FRAME is shown in photo above. Panel A is top; B is the back panel; C and F are end panels; D and E are the two center dividers.

This long and low chest makes a fine stage for a doll line-up and a cozy seat for the children. The colorful upholstered pad is optional but makes a comfortable perch and protects the top.

Because several 3/4-inch dado and rabbet cuts are needed in the construction of this chest, a power saw with dado blade is almost a necessity. The chest shown is made of glued-up redwood panels, but 3/4-inch plywood can be used (edges must be treated, see page 85).

To make the frame, cut out top, back, side, and center panels and make rabbet and dado grooves as shown. Apply glue to rabbet at back of top panel and nail top to back with small finishing nails. Glue cen-

ter panels in place (you can drive a few nails into these through the back for extra support). Glue six 3/4 by 3 by 23 1/2-inch bracing strips inside front ends of dadoes. Allow glue to set. Glue 12 drawer runners, 2 by 12 1/4 by 3/4-inch, in remainder of interior dadoes. Anchor runners with corrugated fasteners.

Drawer fronts measure 6 3/4 by 23 inches (and are of the same 3/4-inch material). Check and fit them for size before continuing. To make hand holes, drill 3 adjoining holes with 1-inch bit, then file and sand to shape.

To make drawers, see page 91. Sides are 1/2 by 6 by 14 3/4 inches, backs are 1/2 by 5 1/4 by 22 inches. Cut drawer bottom from 1/4-inch plywood or hardboard.

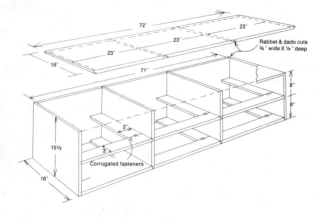

Baby's cabinet today...later, a desk

This cabinet is designed for a baby's needs—both present and future. It provides a big counter for changing the baby at a comfortable height and it has generous storage space below for baby's clothes and toys.

When the child is older, the cabinet can be taken apart to become a pair of play desks, and the two large lower drawers stacked together to form a chest of drawers. Or, half of the cabinet can be used sooner as a smaller changing counter, and the other half used by an older child as a work counter, play desk, and storage chest.

Construction is quite simple. All four sections are made of ³/₄-inch plywood with ¹/₄-inch plywood backs rabbeted into the sides. (For information on working with plywood, see page 84.)

Drawers are sturdily built, as shown, in a standard kitchen-drawer type of construction (for alternative drawer plans, see page 91). All assembly is done with nails and white glue. The four sections are finished in non-toxic enamels.

Design: L. Law.

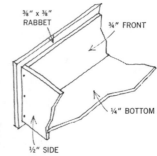

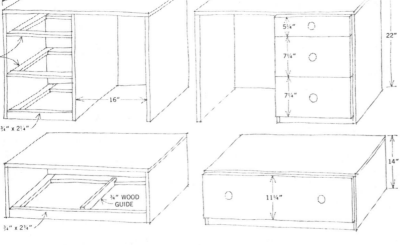

RABBET all four sides of drawer fronts to overlap chest frame ³/₈-inch.

OUTDOOR FURNITURE

Most of the construction techniques used in making indoor furniture can be applied to outdoor furniture, but there are some distinct advantages and disadvantages to building for the outdoors. Outdoor furniture usually has a rustic quality that helps it blend in with its surroundings. As a result, the home craftsman can be less concerned with concealing joints, nails or screws, and with exactness of fit. In addition, outdoor furniture is usually built of softwood, which is less expensive and easier to work than hardwood. For these reasons, it is logical for the inexperienced furniture builder to begin with some of the projects in this section. In making furniture for the outdoors, remember that weather will take its toll. Hardware should be galvanized or non-rusting to prevent staining of the wood. Some softwoods age gracefully without finishes (redwood, cedar, and cypress), but unprotected surfaces absorb grease and dirt stains and rapidly weather. Use a water repellent or sealer as well as a hard finish to protect the wood from the elements. Also, remember to use resorcin resin or another waterproof glue, rather than standard white glue.

Lounge chair

This canvas chair (see front cover) is simple and direct in both concept and construction. Built inexpensively in only a few hours, it is ideal for either patio or indoor use. The one shown is of fir and redwood, but you may use hardwood for additional strength and elegance.

Side frames are laminated with overlapping corners for strength and beauty, and the light Douglas fir on the outside contrasts with the darker redwood centers to dramatize the laminations. Three 1³/₄-inch dowels connect the two end sections and provide support for the canvas sling. Short dowels in the top front corners balance the design.

To make the chair, first cut all pieces as shown in the illustration. Carefully glue end-sections together with resorcinol or epoxy glue, taking special care around corners. Use clamps or small finishing nails to help join the laminations (countersink and fill any nails). Three-inch metal corner brackets are used underneath each of the four corners for added strength. An optional crossbar of doweling can be added between front and back legs for even greater rigidity (see illustration).

So that the chair back will provide comfortable support and cushioning, saw the dowel flat (see illustration) and tuck a piece of firm, inch-thick polyurethane foam into the top loop of canvas around the dowel.

The three-looped canvas sling can be made on any sewing machine. You'll need 2¹/₂ yards of 29-inch-wide chair duck and a spool of heavy-duty thread.

Cut duck to an 86-inch-long piece. Loop the duck and make a ¹/₂-inch seam on the 29-inch edge using heavy-duty thread (see diagram). Then make another row of stitching close to the first row, or make a flat-fell seam for extra strength. You now have an 85-inch-diameter loop.

Form three loops as shown in diagram. Loops will be a little larger than the finished dimensions shown; this leaves room for stitching. Space the three rows of stitching about ¹/₄-inch apart.

Design: Rick Morrall.

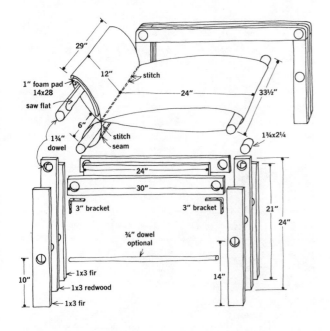

FRONT CORNER PLUG is just decorative. Round corners and edges using a rasp or wood file.

Ideas for outdoor benches

Making an outdoor bench is a logical starting point for the beginning furniture builder. Design and construction of a garden bench is often very basic—even rough —but a good introduction to working with building materials.

Bench seats are usually wood (redwood, pine, fir, cedar, or cypress) but many other rot and termite-proof materials such as pipe, angle iron, flat iron, brick, concrete block, and flue tile can be used for legs.

For wooden seats, use 2-inch-thick lumber for strength. You can also use 1 by 2's or 1 by 3's if you set them on edge. Be sure thick lumber, such as 2 by 8's or 2 by 10's, is well seasoned to avoid warpage or splits. Leave a ¼ to ½-inch space between boards on bench seats to allow for expansion, and for rain water to drain through.

Comfortable height for most benches is between 15 and 18 inches; width should be about 14 to 24 inches. The length, of course, depends upon where you plan to use it. To avoid sagging, space legs about 3 to 5 feet apart—closer if you use light lumber.

Bench at right is 6 feet long and two feet wide. The seat is made from 2 by 2 lumber, spaced evenly apart with 1-inch blocks over the legs. The legs are ¼ by 4-inch flat iron painted black, bolted to two 2 by 4's under the bench. A 2 by 2 frame is mitered around the seat.
Design: Paul Weissich.

Concrete blocks form the bases of these two benches. Nail two 1 by 3's across four evenly-spaced 2 by 4's (ten inches from each end). Epoxy-cement concrete blocks to the 1 by 3's and cement a matching 1 by 3 to the base of each block. Let dry thoroughly before turning right-side up.
Design: Dexter Williams.

Easily moved around to follow the crowd, this L-shaped patio bench was originally built to fit into corners. The photos at right show two positions in which the bench is especially handy.

Fashioned from redwood, you can build one like it in a single afternoon. To make the seat, you will need two 6-foot-long 2 by 6's and one 6-foot-long 2 by 4. Legs are also cut from 2 by 6—each leg is 13³/₄ inches long, so add about 56 inches of 2 by 6 to the two 6-foot lengths needed for the seat. Underbracing requires an additional 5 feet of 2 by 4.

To make full use of the lumber, cut seat as indicated in the drawing. Bevel the ends of the underbracing as shown.

Design: Mildred Davis.

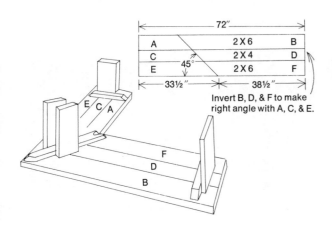

SIMPLE PATIO BENCH can be moved around to fit two different types of corners in your patio.

REDWOOD SLAT BENCH is ideal for patio or terrace. Its open design lets rain drain off quickly to help resist weathering.

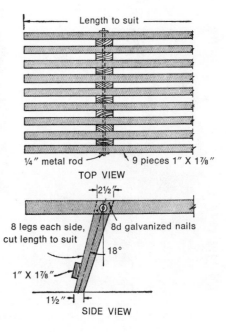

TOP VIEW

¼" metal rod   9 pieces 1" X 1⅞"

8 legs each side, cut length to suit   8d galvanized nails

18°

1" X 1⅞"

1½"

SIDE VIEW

Easy-to-assemble chair, hammock

A good deal of outdoor relaxation can be yours with a minimum investment of time and effort. These lounges can be assembled easily in one afternoon.

Both are made from heavy cotton duck and pipe. The frame of the deck chair shown on this page is made from steel pipe and 2 by 4 lumber. The hammock on the opposite page makes use of plastic sprinkler pipe as a covering for steel pipe. Both the deck chair and hammock are suspended from above.

The swinging deck chair (shown below) hangs from a sturdy overhead beam—yours can hang from a pipe or a good-sized tree limb. You can adjust its height or backrest angle by simply taking up or letting out the lengths of supporting chain. If you hang it horizontally, it becomes a hammock for napping.

To make it, cut two 53½-inch lengths of pine or fir 2 by 4. Cut the corners off and slightly round the edges with a file or sandpaper. In each board, drill a 1¼-inch-diameter hole about 2 inches in from each end.

The sides are made of two 78-inch lengths of 1¼-inch galvanized pipe. Drill a ¼-inch hole about 1 inch in from each end of the pipes for an eye bolt. The seat slings are made from 3 pieces of heavy marine canvas, 31 by 66 inches. These slings have 3-inch side hems for strength and looped ends for the pipes to pass through. Hang the hammock with 1½-inch-link chain.

Design: Graham A. Davey.

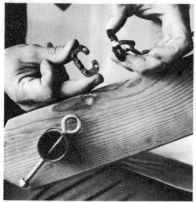

SPLIT LINK CONNECTORS make adjusting chains an easy job.

EYE BOLTS go through pipe and hold wooden ends in place.

To make the plastic pipe hammock,
you will need heavy duck, sprinkler pipe, dacron thread and rope, and some hardware. You will have to visit several different suppliers:
Awning maker. Buy 3¼ yards of 36-inch-wide No. 8 chair duck.
Ship chandlery. Buy a spool of dacron thread and about 24 feet of ½-inch dacron rope.
Plumbing supply store. For the frame, buy 20 feet of 1-inch 80-gauge rigid PVC plastic pipe, four 1-inch 90° elbows, and a small can of PVC solvent. Also buy 20 feet of ¾-inch steel pipe to reinforce the frame.
Hardware store. Buy the two shackles, two hooks, chain, and plastic tubing for hanging the hammock.

Cut the fabric as diagramed at right to make the main body and 10 bands. Discard the extra fabric.

Turn under ½-inch of a narrow end of the hammock body. Using dacron thread and a heavy-duty sewing machine needle, stitch, fold under 3½ inches, and topstitch in place. Always make several rows of stitching, or backstitch over, to secure the ends. Repeat at the other end.

Hem the long edges of the bands. Beginning about 7 inches from each looped hammock end, space five bands evenly along both long edges of the hammock (see diagram), placing right side of bands against right side of hammock. The bands should be about a foot apart and ¾-inch in from the long edges.

Stitch through the two thicknesses (band and hammock) nearest the hammock edge. Fold free end of each band back toward the outer edge. Make several rows of topstitching close to the fold line.

Hem free end of band. Pin on wrong side of fabric about 2 inches in from the hammock edge to form a loop. (Most home sewing machines won't sew through more than three thicknesses of duck; that's why this band edge must be set well in.) Topstitch two or more rows to add strength. Repeat on all the bands. A sail repair kit can be used to resew any pulled stitches by hand.

To make the frame, use a hacksaw to cut both the metal and plastic pipes into two 7-foot lengths and

two 3-foot lengths. Slide the metal pipe inside the plastic pipe. Slip the double pipe through the fabric loops.

Place hammock assembly on top of papers to protect floor against dripping solvent. Following label directions, apply solvent to elbow and pipe and quickly assemble. Repeat on all the corners, making sure the elbows and pipes are flat on the floor as you glue them. Leave undisturbed for the recommended length of time.

This hammock is suspended with heavy dacron rope and link chain covered with clear plastic tubing. The chain is joined with shackles; heavy hooks join the chain and rope.

WRAP FREE ENDS of rope with adhesive tape to prevent unraveling.

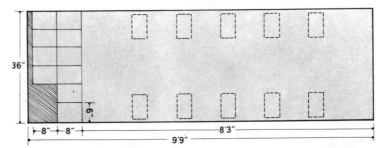

CUT FABRIC along the solid lines and discard the waste material. Dotted lines show first position of the side bands.

Rolling patio pallets

These patio pallets lead a double life. As individual seats, they can be rolled around to follow the crowd. Joined up in a string of three, they form a comfortable lounge for sunbathing by the pool. Since they're so easy to build, you may want to make several sets.

The polyurethane cushions shown were made at an upholstery shop dealing in foam rubber. Edges and one side are covered with a white vinyl cloth-backed fabric, easily cleaned with a damp cloth. The other side is white duck (cooler for sunbathing). Cushions are 23 inches square and 4 inches thick. If you use lightweight material, you can sew the covers on a home machine.

To make three pallets, you'll need a half-sheet (4-foot square) of 3/4-inch exterior plywood, 26 feet of 1/2 by 6-inch fir, and a dozen 2-inch pivoting casters.

From the 3/4-inch plywood, cut 3 cushion bases, each 24 inches square, and 24 caster-pads 4 1/2 inches square. From the 1/2-inch stock, cut 12 sides 24 inches long (to the inside of the miter at each end); then ripsaw them to 5-inch width. The 5-inch width is suggested for proper proportion. If you choose not to ripsaw, buy standard 1 by 6 lumber (actual dimensions 3/4 by 5 1/2 inches) instead of the 1/2-inch stock.

Using nails and waterproof glue, assemble the seats as sketched below. Glue and nail four *double* caster pads to the underside of each seat. Then mount the casters 2 inches in from the sides.

Paint the pallets in bright enamel. If you plan more than one set, contrasting colors will make them even more lively.

Design: Gordon Hammond.

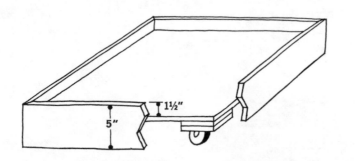

1 1/2"

5"

Adjustable chaise for sun-basking

One great pleasure of summer is basking in the sun on a full-length chaise. This updated classic is comfortable and sturdy, but light looking. It rolls about the patio on concealed casters. The backrest is adjustable, and the slender shape of the lounge requires very little space for off-season storage.

To make the chaise, you will need one sheet of ½-inch exterior plywood, two 8-foot lengths of 1 by 4 fir, two 6-foot lengths of 1 by 1, and 4 feet of 1 by 2. You will also need 4 feet of piano hinge with screws, six 2½-inch casters, and a standard 2 by 6-foot *chaise longue* pad (purchased from an outdoor furniture store).

From the plywood, cut the 24 by 48-inch main base, the 24-inch-square grooved base, the 23¾ by 24-inch backrest, the 8¾ by 23¾-inch backrest prop, and eight 4-inch-square caster pads (see "Working with Plywood," on pages 84-85).

Cut ¼-inch-deep, 9/16-inch-wide grooves in the grooved base about 1⅜ inches apart, starting eight inches from the inside (hinged) end. With a saber saw (or drill and keyhole saw), cut a 1 by 4-inch finger hole in the backrest prop. Sand all rough edges.

From the 1 by 4 fir, cut two side strips 77½ inches long. From the 1 by 1 lumber, cut four rails: two 47 inches, two 23 inches. From the 1 by 2, cut one end strip 24 inches, the other 23¾ inches.

Using galvanized nails and waterproof glue, attach the 1 by 1-inch rails to the side strips as in the sketch. The short rails fit flush with the bottom of the side strip. Nail and glue the 23¾-inch end strip to the backrest, the 24-inch end strip to the base, and the two bases to the rails. Using a 23¾-inch piano hinge, attach the backrest prop to the backrest 11 inches from the base hinge end. Then attach the backrest to the base with another 23¾-inch piano hinge. Nail and glue caster pads to base as sketch shows. Install casters with screws.

Paint the finished chaise with three coats of enamel, lightly sanding in between.

Design: Gordon Hammond.

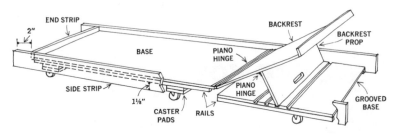

CHAISE accommodates standard 2 by 6-foot pad. End and side strips hold it in place. Base is grooved for backrest prop.

TO SIT UP, adjust hinged backrest to any of the four different lounging positions.

This charpoy (pronounced "shar-poy") is modeled after the common bed or cot of India and Pakistan.

Feel free to be casual with the design. Charpoys are made in all sizes and heights. Some are only half the length shown and serve as chairs. All have two definite characteristics: the simple wood framing and the open rope lashing at the foot end. This allows you to weave the stringing quite loosely and then pull it taut with the rope lashing (and retighten if it sags).

The stringing also varies. Some are woven of reeds or cane. This charpoy is woven with a common polished wrapping twine called India cord, and requires five 300-foot rolls.

You will need 1³/₄-inch hardwood doweling or 2-inch-square hardwood lumber for the rails.

You can use square stock for the legs, or specially shape them. The rails are joined to legs with 1-inch doweling.

For the stringing, make a simple wooden needle (as shown) to ease weaving. At the start, you can weave with just the ball of twine, but as strands fill up the space, it becomes easier to weave with 30-foot lengths of twine tied to the needle. Tie each new piece to the last with a square knot and leave 2-inch ends so they will hang. Lash about 15 feet of ¼-inch Manila twine at the foot end before beginning to weave (pull this taut when finished). Weave initial strand over and under itself (see illustration) until full pattern is completed. Repeat four times.

A woven cot

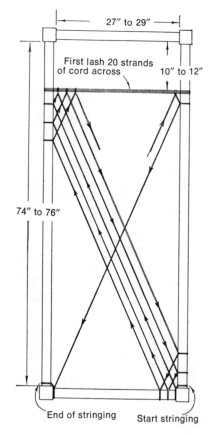

27" to 29"

First lash 20 strands of cord across

10" to 12"

74" to 76"

End of stringing   Start stringing

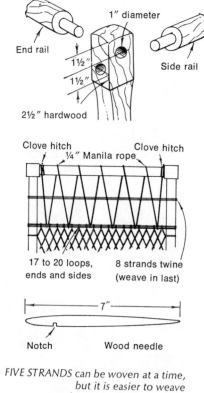

End rail

1" diameter

1½"

1½"

Side rail

2½" hardwood

Clove hitch   Clove hitch

¼" Manila rope

17 to 20 loops, ends and sides

8 strands twine (weave in last)

7"

Notch   Wood needle

FIVE STRANDS can be woven at a time, but it is easier to weave one strand completely through the simple pattern, then repeat.

Fold-up table has three levels

This three-in-one table serves equally well on a picnic, on the patio, and inside the house. You can adjust it to heights of 16, 24, and 28 inches simply by altering the position of the legs. The low position is best for display of potted plants on the patio or for beach use. At middle height, it can be a children's table or a coffee table. In the high position, it becomes a dining or game table for adults.

Made from vertical grain fir, the one shown was built in a home workshop in about 4 hours.

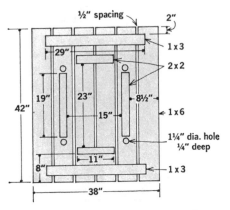

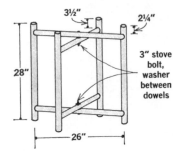

MULTI-USE TABLE can be used at three different levels, the lowest is at left. To get middle position, you turn leg assembly 90° and fit legs against opposite stops. Set legs on end for full height.

Wood slabs make a patio table

Meant to seat eight, this handsome outdoor table can be used either for dining or as a buffet. It's light enough to pick up and move, so you can place it where you like, in sun or shade. You may even want to use it in your dining room.

The table is made entirely of surfaced 2 by 10 and 2 by 12-inch stock. If intended for outdoor use, redwood or cedar are recommended. You will need one 6-foot and four 10-foot lengths of 2 by 10, plus 12 feet of 2 by 12. The overall length of the table is 7 feet; the width is equal to four 2 by 10's—about 38 inches.

To form the top, cut the right pieces as shown in the sketch and bevel the four outside boards. Assemble the tabletop using blind dowel joints (see page 89). Use waterproof glue only on diagonal joints.

To make the pedestal bases, cut two pieces from the 6-foot length of 2 by 10. Then cut four pieces from the 12 feet of 2 by 12. Make a 60° cut on these four pieces. Bevel the opposite end of each piece as shown in the sketch. Assemble each pedestal using galvanized finishing nails and waterproof glue. (A power saw is the best tool for this operation, but you can mark and cut it by hand.)

Turn the table upside down. Use blind dowels with glue to attach pedestals. Let glue dry before turning the table upright.

The wood grain is enhanced by the diagonal pattern-cuts of the tabletop. If you would like to keep the natural beauty of the wood, leave the table unpainted and unvarnished. To turn the wood a warm buckskin color, apply two coats of water repellent. Left to itself, the wood will then gradually weather, becoming ever greyer. To retain the buckskin shade, use water repellent as often as necessary.

Design: Mark Mills.

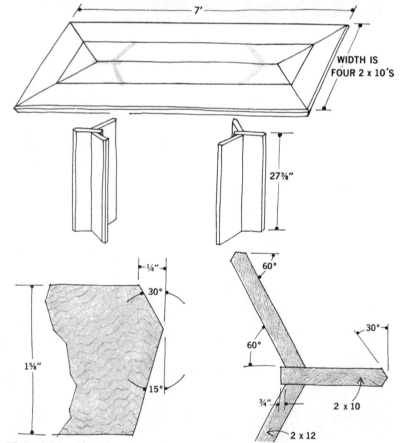

BEVEL SIDE and end pieces with two saw cuts. Lightly sand surfaces.

CUT BASE of two legs at 60° angle. Finish each member with 30° bevels.

This table is wobble proof

This three-legged table will stand firmly on any kind of surface. Unlike many four-legged tables, it has proved wobble-proof on redwood decks, flagstone floors, concrete-block paving, and lawns.

Six adults can sit around this hex-agonal table with ample leg room, even though its diameter is only 50 inches. The table is lightweight and easy to move anywhere it's needed. Also shown is a matching bench that will seat two.

To make the table, first lay out the tabletop on a large sheet of paper. Using a yardstick as a compass, mark a circle with a 25-inch radius. Then use the same compass to mark off points around the circumference that are 25 inches (in a straight line) from each other; these will be the corners of the hexagon.

Lay the six 2 by 8 boards on top, spacing them about 1/2-inch apart—or whatever is needed to make them come out even. Mark and cut the boards.

Assemble the entire top with its 2 by 3 trim. Taper the three legs, bolt them to three rails with 5/16 or 3/8-inch bolts (checking before assembly to make sure they fit), and nail or screw the rail-leg assembly to the underside of the top.

Construction of the bench is shown in the sketch below.

Design: Clifford M. Hickman.

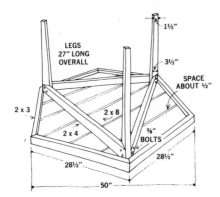

UPSIDE-DOWN VIEW shows the 3-legged table's simple construction.

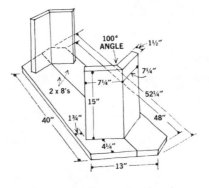

USE GLUE as well as nails, dowels, or metal angles to attach legs.

Flue-tile table

For those who wish to make patio furniture with a minimum of cost and effort, chimney-flue tile offers some pleasant possibilities. Its color and proportion blend well with outdoor surroundings and it is relatively inexpensive.

The two tables shown here may be constructed with only a hammer, handsaw, and screwdriver. The coffee table is supported by 8½ by 13-inch tiles, while the dining table is set on the 13 by 13-inch size. Both tabletops are made from 1 by 6-inch redwood with a finished dimension of 30 by 72 inches. The dining table has 1 by 2-inch cleats to keep the top from sliding and uses angle irons bolted to each tile and screwed to the top to give additional stability (drill hole with pointed rattail file or star drill). You can also attach the angle irons with epoxy glue.

Table top

Flue lining

1 X 2

Angle iron

Screw

¼" bolt

BILL OF MATERIALS

Coffee Table
2 flue tiles 18½" x 13" x 25" for legs
1 x 6 redwood—total length 30'
  5 pcs. 6' long for tabletop
1 x 2 redwood—total length 7'6"
  3 pcs. 30" long for cleats
3 doz. 1½" wood screws

Dining Table
2 flue tiles 13" x 13" x 25" for legs
1 x 6 redwood—total length 30'
  5 pcs. 6' long for top
1 x 2—total length 16'6"
  3 pcs 30" long for cleats
  6 pcs. 18" long for cleats
¼" carriage bolts 2½" long
6 doz. 1½" wood screws
2 angle braces 2" long

Plywood table

One 4 by 8 foot sheet of ¾-inch plywood is all you need to make this very easily constructed table. It is attractive, inexpensive, and versatile enough to be used either in or out of doors. The table shown is made from exterior-grade fir plywood, since it's intended primarily for outdoors. For indoor use, you may prefer a hardwood-faced plywood (see page 84 for plywood types). If you don't paint the table, treat all plywood edges (see page 85).

After making four saw-cuts with a power saw or handsaw, cut four notches (see plan) with either a saber saw or a spiral-toothed blade in a coping saw. Assemble the table by locking legs and brace into each other and attaching top with angle iron or metal corner brackets (using ⅝-inch screws). To make the table demountable for easy carrying and flat storage, omit corner brackets, angle iron, and screws. Then nail four wooden cleats to the underside to help center it and hold it in place.

Design: Fred Langhorst.

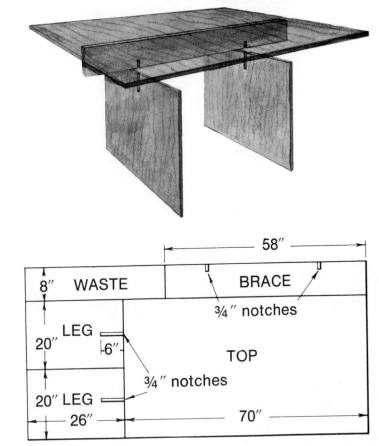

Plan dimensions: 58″, 8″ WASTE, BRACE, ¾″ notches, LEG 20″, 6″, TOP, ¾″ notches, 20″ LEG, 26″, 70″

Barbecue table set

This barbecue set is surely a familiar sight to anyone who has ever dined outdoors. The popularity of this particular design is due not only to its attractive appearance, but also to its sturdiness, simple construction to any size desired, and demountable members for compact storage. The design can be easily modified by increasing the length of the top and seat boards to add to seating space without altering other dimensions. The redwood pieces are secured with lag screws and bolts so that the unit may be dismantled for storing during the winter months.

Design: Middlekauff Mfg. Co.

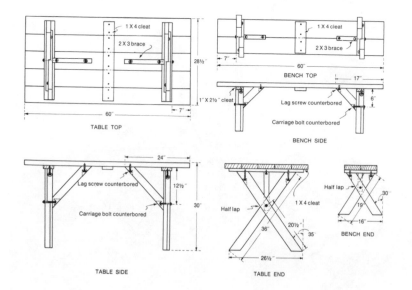

TABLE TOP

1 X 4 cleat
2 X 3 brace
28½"
60"
7"
1" X 2½" cleat

BENCH TOP

1 X 4 cleat
2 X 3 brace
60"
7"
17"

BENCH SIDE

Lag screw counterbored
Carriage bolt counterbored
6"

TABLE SIDE

24"
12½"
30"
Lag screw counterbored
Carriage bolt counterbored

TABLE END

Half lap
1 X 4 cleat
36"
20½"
26½"
35"

BENCH END

Half lap
30
19
16"

BILL OF MATERIALS

2 x 6 redwood—total length 45'

  9 pcs. 60" long for table and bench top

2 x 4 redwood—total length 25'4"

  4 pcs. 36" long for table legs

  8 pcs. 19" long for bench legs

2 x 3 redwood—total length 7'8"

  2 pcs. 24" long for table braces

  4 pcs. 11" long for bench braces

1 x 4 redwood—total length 12'

  3 pcs. 26" long for cleats

  6 pcs. 10½" long for cleats

54 wood screws 2" long

8 ¼" x 3½" lag screws

6 ⅜" x 6" carriage bolts

All from one sheet of plywood

You can make this 44-inch-diameter table and the four 20-inch stools—legs and all—from just one 4 by 8-foot sheet of ¾-inch plywood. The stools alone can serve as occasional tables at a party.

The cost is minimal, and will depend on the plywood you choose. For outdoor use, buy exterior plywood, so that the wood will not delaminate in the rainy season (it will still need a sealer and finishing coat).

Mark the plywood as illustrated, then cut out all pieces, preferably with a saber saw. Actually, you may use any type of saw to cut the 48-inch square for the table and the 24-inch squares for the stools, but you should then cut the legs from the square pieces with a bandsaw, jigsaw, or coping saw (see page 84 for tips on cutting plywood).

Attach the legs according to either method shown below by drilling holes through the legs and screwing them onto the tops (using glue as additional reinforcement). In the method at bottom left, you notch pairs of legs. This produces legs that extend out beyond the tops, reminiscent of early California furniture. But, by cutting through the legs (bottom right) and lapping them together, you can assemble them to fit entirely under the tabletop.

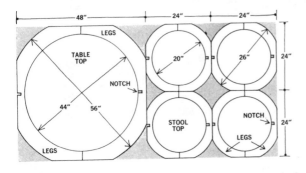

TWO PAIRS OF LEGS, notched at center, are put together, glued, and screwed to the seat.

ALTERNATE METHOD. Legs can be cut separately, shortened, and attached to the seat as shown here.

BUILDING AND FINISHING TIPS

Before you begin the actual construction of a piece of furniture, it's a good idea to have a basic knowledge of certain products, tools, and techniques. Familiarity with building materials will enable you to make proper selections for your project—and you can use materials other than those specified in plans if you are aware of their advantages and shortcomings. Although you may be reasonably adept at working with basic hand tools, check out the various types of power tools that can save you time and effort. Also, make it a point to learn how to put together basic furniture elements such as tabletops, drawers, and cabinet doors. The section that follows is intended as a quick-reference guide to some of the most important aspects of furniture building—from selection of the materials to applying the final finish.

Things you should know about lumber

Many different types of wood are used in furniture making. Each type has inherent qualities that affect its workability, appearance, and durability. These qualities, plus the availability of the wood and its condition when purchased, usually determine its cost. Most furniture items can be made from any one of a number of woods—the type you select will be the strongest factor in the ultimate cost of your project.

Hardwood or Softwood

Woods are divided into two broad categories: hardwoods and softwoods. These terms can be misleading; they refer to the kind of tree the wood comes from, not the characteristics of the wood. Hardwoods come from broadleafed (deciduous) trees, softwoods from evergreens (conifers). For this reason, some softwoods—like yew and Douglas fir—are actually harder than so-called hardwoods like poplar, aspen, and Philippine mahogany. Balsa, the softest of woods, is technically a hardwood.

Hardwood is generally more expensive than softwoods. Mistakes in working with it can be relatively costly—a careless saw cut that might spoil a dollar's worth of redwood (softwood) will ruin two or three times that investment in oak (hardwood).

Nevertheless, furniture builders often prefer hardwood, not only for its natural beauty but because it lends itself to precision workmanship. Though usually more difficult to work than softwood, hardwood responds handsomely to careful tooling. Satin-smooth surfaces and hairline joints can be the rewards of the conscientious handyman.

Unlike the highly standardized dimensions of common softwoods (see inside front cover), hardwood is sold in odd lengths and sizes, usually unsurfaced. Knowing how to order both types of wood properly can save you money.

Almost all softwoods are easy to nail; most hardwood requires special fastening techniques. It is too tough to drive a nail through—if the wood doesn't split, the nail doubles over. Therefore, holes must be drilled for nails as well as screws. The most commonly used "fastener" for hardwood furniture is glue—it has the great advantage of eliminating unsightly nail holes while, at the same time, it offers a strong bond. When using nails and screws as fasteners, use glue for

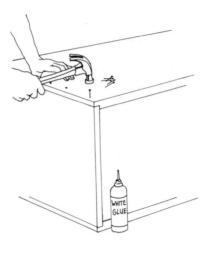

added strength unless you want the joint to be demountable. Remember to allow extra time for the completion of a piece of furniture when you use glue.

How Lumber Is Graded

Grading standards differ for hardwood and softwood (for softwood grading standards, see inside front cover).

Hardwood grading is complex and is governed by standards set by the National Hardwood Lumber Association. There are some general rules, but each variety of wood has special requirements. Grading is based on the number of cuts necessary to produce a given size of lumber. The permissible defects, such as

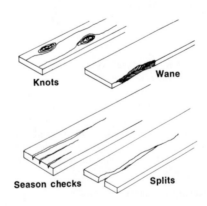

Knots   **Wane**

Season checks   **Splits**

knots, wane, splits, season checks, and others, vary with each grade.

"Firsts" and "Seconds" are the top two grades of hardwood lumber. These are usually combined into one grade—

called "FAS." Unless specified otherwise, orders are usually filled with FAS. "Selects" is the third grade of hardwood lumber, followed by "Number 1 Common," "Number 2 Common," "Sound Wormy," "Number 3A Common," and "Number 3B Common." Both sides of a board are graded; a grade in which only the best side meets FAS requirements is "FAS 1 face."

An Aid to Ordering Lumber

All wood is sold by the board foot, the lineal foot, and, in some cases, by the pound. The dimensions given for thickness and width of a board are figured before drying or finishing, so the actual dimensions of the lumber you buy will be somewhat less.

If you want enough hardwood to do a particular job, it will cost less if you simply specify the footage you need. The lumberman will sell you what he has in stock that fills your requirement with least waste. As a general rule, figure about 1/3 extra for waste. To cut cost, always order the smallest pieces that will do the job.

When ordering, specify whether you want the material air-dried or kiln-dried—this will depend on the wood and how you intend to use it. All wood for cabinet work should be kiln-dried to reduce warpage and shrinkage. Your dealer will help you decide whether you need kiln-dried stock for the job you have in mind.

You can buy lumber either rough or surfaced. If you have a jointer or planer in your workshop, you can do your own surfacing and save money. If you don't have a planer, it is best to order surfaced material; it costs less to buy it already surfaced than to buy it rough and then have it finished in a cabinet shop.

Hardwood is often sold with two sides surfaced, or surfaced on two sides with one edge squared to give you an alignment corner to work from.

When writing an order for hardwood, list the following items: number of pieces; kind of wood; grain—color or figure; size—thickness, width, length; grade, seasoning, and millwork. Example: 10 pcs. Phil. mahogany, dark red; 7/8" net x 10" x 6'0"; FAS, KD, S2S. This means you need ten 6-foot-long pieces of dark red Philippine mahogany, 7/8-inch in thickness (after surfacing) and 10 inches wide, FAS-grade, kiln-dried, surfaced on 2 sides.

Plywood and hardwood

Several types of superior wood products have been developed by modern technology. The majority are wooden "sheet" materials—flat sheets of laminated or compressed wood products that are generally stronger, more flexible, and less likely to split than ordinary lumber. They expand and contract less than common lumber and are available in large sizes (usually 4 by 8-foot sheets) that would be impossible to mill and distribute in the wood's natural form. They are sometimes available in half sheets (4 by 4 feet) or odd sizes. All of these products fall under the categories of either plywood or hardboard.

Kinds of Plywood

In effect, plywood is a sandwich panel of real wood, made from an odd number of thin sheets of wood laid with the grain running in alternate directions and bonded under pressure, glues, and sometimes heat. There are several types available to the home craftsman that are excellent for the construction of furniture.

Softwood plywood. Douglas fir plywood is the least expensive and most commonly found type. It is available in two types—interior and exterior—depending upon the gluebond and grade of veneer.

The inner plies of exterior plywood are all of high quality and bonded together with a completely waterproof glue. This type of plywood will resist time and weather—even when boiled in water it will not delaminate. Interior plywood is water-resistant but not waterproof, so should not be included in projects for permanent outdoor use.

All fir plywoods (particularly rotary cut types) have a tendency to check when used outdoors. These should never be used outdoors with only a stain because of the maintenance problems. Checking can be reduced by careful painting with a conventional three-coat paint system. Edges should be daubed with a heavy coat of primer or a thick mixture of white lead and oil. Warping may become another problem, but is less likely to occur if the panels are stored in a dry place and finished identically on both sides.

Standard fir plywood thicknesses are $1/4$, $3/8$, $1/2$, $5/8$ and $3/4$-inch. Some large lumber distributors also carry $1\frac{1}{8}$-inch.

Quality of face and back panels determine the grading of fir plywood. Letters A, B, C, and D indicate the different grades. A is the best quality, B is smooth (excellent for painting), C has knotholes and splits, and D is the poorest (often used for inner plys of interior plywood). Two letters are used in the grading of a sheet of plywood—one for the face and one for the back. Where only one side will show, it is economical to use A-D, with one good side. For further information on grading of plywood, see inside front cover.

Hardwood-faced plywood. Most hardwoods are available in plywood form. If you can use hardwood-faced plywood for a project instead of solid lumber, the savings will be considerable (particularly with the more expensive woods). What you are actually buying is a thin veneer (sometimes only 1/28-inch) of the hardwood, glued to a core of less expensive wood. Standard sheet sizes are 4 by 8 feet.

Grading of hardwood-faced plywood is different from that used for fir plywood. For making furniture, choose *Custom* or *Good*.

Like fir plywood, the hardwood-faced variety is available in both interior and exterior panels.

Lumber-core plywood. Made primarily for fine cabinet work, these panels are made with inner cores of edge-laminated strips of wood, rather than the sheets used in common plywood. When using hardwood-faced plywood, cabinetmakers often choose lumber-core panels over the usual veneer types because they are more stable and less likely to warp. Though these panels often don't require special edge treatment, they are easy to work with where it *is* needed.

Grooved (Texture 1-11) plywood. Specially-grooved $3/8$-inch dado cuts run the length of these fir plywood panels, spaced apart from each other at 2, 4, or 8-inch centers. Although an exterior-type plywood, it is excellent for use indoors where a special textured effect is desired. It is also a natural for adjustable bookshelves (see page 27).

Resin-overlaid fir plywood. This type consists of standard exterior-grade fir plywood with sheets of resin-impregnated paper permanently fused to the wood. It offers an excellent surface to paint on, since grain raise and checking do not show. High-density panels are attractive even when left unfinished.

Hardboard-veneered plywood. The good qualities of two competitive materials are utilized in hardboard-veneered plywood. Sheets of $1/8$-inch hardboard are laminated onto both sides of ordinary panels of fir plywood. The plywood provides strength, while the hardboard supplies a perfectly smooth, check-free painting surface. The product is useful for interior or exterior cabinet-work where a smooth, paintable surface is desired.

Working with Plywood

The biggest job when working with plywood is usually cutting the large panels to size. If you will be cutting several panels from a full-sized sheet of plywood, as most of the plans in this book call for, it's a good idea to draw the sections on a piece of paper and transfer the marks onto the plywood. Always double-check measurements to be sure they are correct, and don't forget to allow for the saw kerf (width of cut) between pieces. If you plan to cut the piece with a handsaw, power radial or table saw, mark on the better face of the plywood and cut it with this side up. If using a portable power saw, mark and cut the panel from the back side. Plan to reduce the sheets to workable size with the first cuts.

Power saws are great for cutting plywood. Radial, table, and portable power saws are extremely helpful in cutting straight lines. Jigsaws, bandsaws, and saber saws cut curves easily. If you cut plywood by hand, choose a keyhole or coping saw for curves and a handsaw with 10 to 15 teeth-per-inch for straight lines. Special plywood blades with fine, shallow-set teeth can be purchased for power saws, to aid in making clean cuts. Be sure all saw blades are sharp.

There are several methods used to

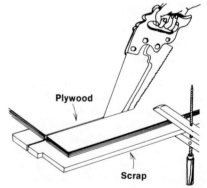

Plywood

Scrap

help prevent plywood undersides from splitting-out when being cut. Both sides of the panel can be scribed through the top veneer along the cut-off line with a sharp knife or chisel. Or, you can carefully tape along bottom side of cut-off line with cellophane tape. When hand-sawing, put a piece of scrap lumber under plywood and saw both together.

To keep wood from splitting-out when boring holes, either clamp a piece of wood on the back of the plywood or turn it over as soon as the point of the bit appears through the backside and finish drilling from the back.

To plane plywood edges (a job that isn't usually necessary), work from both ends toward the center using a sharp, shallow-set blade. If possible, cut a tiny bevel at each corner to help prevent edges from splitting-out.

Sanding surfaces of plywood is not necessary—it only removes soft grain. When sanding edges, use 80-grit (or finer) sandpaper.

Covering Plywood Edges

Plywood, because of its rough, laminated edges, should be used in the place of solid lumber for furniture construction only when edges can be covered. There are several ways to disguise plywood edges.

A matching strip of solid wood can be glued and graded to the edge in either

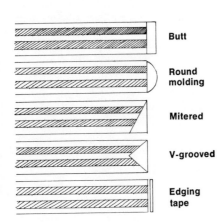

Butt

Round molding

Mitered

V-grooved

Edging tape

mitered, butt, or V-grooved fashion. Screen moldings, commonly stocked by lumber dealers, can be fastened in the same way for a fancier edge. You can also buy edging tape of thin veneered wood with an adhesive backing (available in 8-foot rolls) to match the wood you are working with.

For methods of hiding plywood edges when joining panels, see page 89.

What to Know About Hardboard

One very versatile artificial paneling material is hardboard. Usually quite smooth on one side and screened on the reverse, hardboard is made of wood chips that have been separated into individual fibers then bonded under heat and pressure into sheets of dense wood fiber. For added moisture resistance and strength, some hardboard is tempered with thermal-setting materials baked into place.

Hardboard comes in dark brown, gray, or blond; plain, striated, or perforated. Thicknesses range from 1/10 to 5/16-inch. The thinner types are extremely flexible, and the thicker types can be bent by making a few saw cuts on the reverse side of the bend.

Hardboard's density makes it one of the most dent-resistant of all the panel products—excellent for flat areas that must take wear. The smooth finish is ideal for painting, and will not check or split in weather. Because the fibers are not aligned, the board has strength in all directions.

Problems with hardboard include its inability to hold nails or screws securely; the fact that it expands and contracts with changes in moisture (presenting problems with joints); and its sometimes cold, hard appearance.

In addition to regular hardboard and the two types listed below, you can buy numerous specialized types, such as striated or combed-finish hardboard; plastic-coated types simulating tile, marble, wood grain, and leather; corrugated hardboard; pre-stained hardboard; and painted hardboard.

Perforated hardboard is one of the most popular varieties. It is very good for sliding cabinet doors and stereo-cabinet backs, as it allows air to circulate; or, it can be used for a "hang-up" storage wall (a wide variety of specially-sized hooks and supports that fit into the perforations are available at hardware stores).

Wood particle or "flake boards" are made from particles of wood rather than from refined wood fibers. Chips give a speckled appearance, in contrast to the smooth look of ordinary hardboard. They are made in thicknesses varying from 1/4-inch paneling material up to 3/4-inch boards for more structural uses. Particle boards are made from a number of dif-

ferent wood species including redwood, maple, cedar, pine, fir, and a combination of pine and fir.

Working with Hardboard

You can work hardboard with ordinary shop tools. When hand sawing, use an 8 to 12 teeth-per-inch handsaw and cut

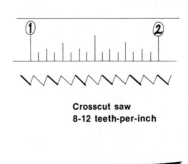

Crosscut saw 8-12 teeth-per-inch

at a fairly flat angle. When cutting with a power saw, use a low-set carbide-tipped combination or crosscut blade—adjusted so that only two or three teeth show through hardboard while cutting. Always cut hardboard with the smooth face up.

Edges can be worked with a shallow-set, sharp plane; a file or rasp (worked lengthwise); or sandpaper. If sanding causes edges to "fuzz-up," control them with a wash coat of shellac before final dressing. Panel surfaces should not be sanded.

Most hardboards can be painted, enameled, stained, waxed, varnished, or lacquered. Unless the material you buy is specially treated and requires no prime coat, always use a good sealer or primer for both interior and exterior work.

Before you paint hardboard, apply one coat of a pigmented or clear resin or penetrating sealer. For a natural finish, you can apply a clear sealer before the wax, lacquer, or varnish finish in order to reduce darkening of the wood.

When working with particle or flake boards, you may want to use a wood paste filler to insure a smooth finish for such items as table and desk tops. Follow the manufacturer's directions in applying the filler, then sand for a perfectly smooth surface. For natural or stained finishes, use a transparent paste filler. Don't use steel wool on untreated particle-finish panels. The fine threads may catch on the individual wood fibers or chips exposed on the surface.

Two useful plastics

Two types of plastic are commonly used in furniture building: acrylic plastic and plastic laminate. Acrylic plastic is used as the principal material in construction of contemporary furniture. Plastic laminate finds use as a hard top for counters and tables.

Acrylic Plastic

Acrylic plastic is rapidly gaining favor as a material for furniture construction. Its popularity is largely due to its clean simplicity and buoyant appearance. Working with the material hardly differs from working with wood. You can buy either translucent or transparent acrylic plastic in sheet form. Almost every color or tint in the rainbow is available, though clear is the most commonly used. Prices vary according to color and thickness of the material. Clear is least expensive but most likely to show scratches under heavy use.

Thicknesses are as varied as colors, but the most commonly used are $1/8$-inch and $1/4$-inch. You can easily work with either. Price difference between $1/4$-inch and $1/8$-inch is minimal.

Some of the tools required for cutting, drilling, bending, finishing edges, and cementing plastic are probably already in your workshop. Even though you may be used to the tools, practice the various operations on scrap material before digging into an actual project.

Cutting. There are several ways to cut acrylic sheet. Thicknesses up to $1/8$-inch can be scored with a scribing tool (similar to a knife) and then broken. Make several passes with the tool along a

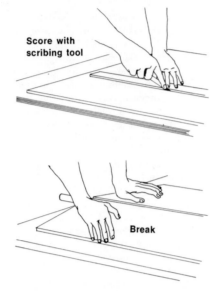

Score with scribing tool

Break

straightedge; run a $3/4$-inch dowel beneath the length of the cut; hold the sheet down firmly with one hand and press with the other on the piece you're cutting off. Your hands should be opposite each other about 2 inches on each side of the intended break. Don't try to break off a piece less than $1 1/2$ inches wide.

A circular saw, with a crosscut blade made for finish cuts on plywood, will deliver very straight cuts in plastic. The blade should have at least 6 teeth-per-inch—all the same height, shape, and dis-

tance from one another. Blade should protrude slightly above the thickness of the plastic. Hold the sheet firmly and cut slowly. Always leave the paper backing on the plastic sheet until you are finished cutting.

Saber, band, and jigsaws will all cut curves easily. The number of teeth-per-inch on the blade is important—saber and jigsaws should have at least 14 teeth-per-inch, band saws at least 10. Hold the plastic securely and don't force the cut.

To drill acrylic sheet, use standard twist bits in either a hand drill or a variable-speed power drill set at low speed. Drill slowly with minimum pres-

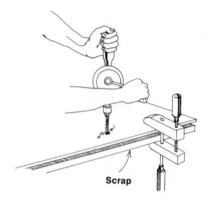

Scrap

sure. Hold or clamp a piece of wood firmly to the back of the plastic sheet to prevent chipping.

Bending. To bend plastic, you will need an electric strip heater. You can put one together for less than $10. Purchase a

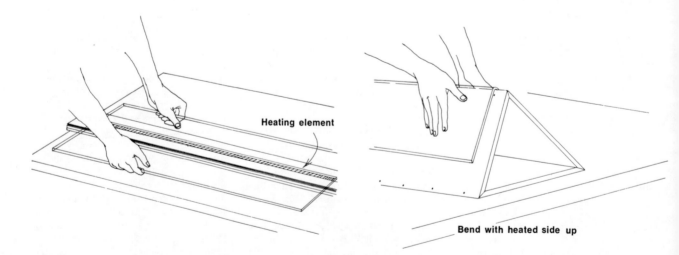

Heating element

Bend with heated side up

BENDING ACRYLIC SHEET

heating element from your plastics dealer and make the rest from odds and ends.

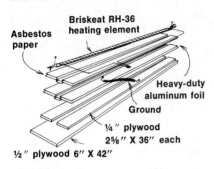

Asbestos paper
Briskeat RH-36 heating element
Heavy-duty aluminum foil
Ground
¼″ plywood 2⅝″ X 36″ each
½″ plywood 6″ X 42″

Before heating, remove masking paper on both surfaces of the plastic. Use a grease pencil to mark for bends. Heat the marked area over the electric element (careful not to touch the coils). Don't heat the plastic over 340 degrees or it may scorch and bubble. If the plastic becomes too hot, widen the distance from the heat source. Allow the plastic to heat until softening occurs (but not bubbles), bend it gently away from the hottest side to the desired angle; then hold firmly until it cools. If you bend the plastic before it's fully heated, small internal fractures will occur along the bend. Practice on scraps to get the feel. Don't attempt to bend sheets thicker than ¼-inch; one side would become very hot, the other not hot enough to bend. It is usually easiest to make complicated bends around a wooden jig (like the one in the sketch on page 15).

Cementing. Joining two pieces together is easy by capillary-cementing with a special solvent (available at plastic outlets). Use a hypodermic oiler, syringe, or eyedropper to apply the solvent to a joint.

Surfaces to be cemented should be sanded but not polished. Tape pieces together for support while glue hardens (about 5 minutes) but be careful not to let solvent run along edges of tape. If solvent accidentally runs onto the surface of a panel, wipe it off quickly to avoid certain marring.

Finishing. Acrylic plastic needs no finishing as such, but should be maintained in good condition. Wash it with mild soap and lukewarm water, then blot dry with a damp cloth or chamois. To help fill in minor scratches and retain the original luster, apply a hard auto wax (not a combination cleaner-wax).

Plastic Laminate

Plastic laminate is an artificial paneling material made of paper layers impregnated with synthetic resins. Panels come in hundreds of colors and patterns, including simulated wood grains. The material's hard surface is extremely resistant to impact, scratches, grease, high temperatures, and moisture.

Although it is an extremely hard material, plastic laminate can break, so be careful when working with it.

A base of ¾-inch plywood is usually mounted under the plastic surface. The plastic is cut to exact size and bonded to the plywood with contact cement.

To cut the plastic, first mark along the cutoff line with a sharp tool (like an awl), then cut along the line at a low angle with a handsaw (12 to 15 teeth-per-inch) or use a power saw with plywood-cutter blade. Cut the panel with the good side

up. Rough edges can be smoothed with sandpaper or file. If you plan to put plastic strips around the sides of the project

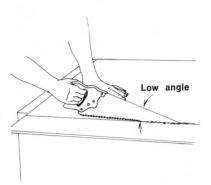

Low angle

top, allow for ⅛-inch overlap on all edges (it is best to cement sides in place before marking top for correct fit).

When the fit is exact, spread contact cement over the back of the panel and on the plywood surface. Follow the adhesive manufacturer's directions, keeping in mind that once the two cemented surfaces touch each other, they cannot be moved. Practice laying the plastic before going on to the cementing.

One method often used to properly position the cemented plastic is to place a large piece of wrapping paper between the cemented plywood and the plastic—to be gradually pulled out as the plastic is pressed into position. Let the cement set in the open about 30 minutes before beginning this operation. Once you start, work slowly and carefully.

When all pieces are together, carefully remove any unevenness at edges or corners with a fine-toothed file.

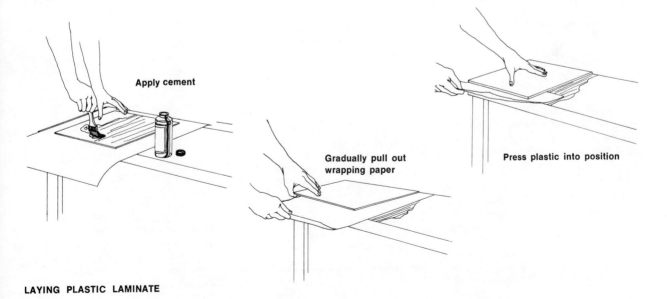

Apply cement

Gradually pull out wrapping paper

Press plastic into position

LAYING PLASTIC LAMINATE

Power tools...for ease and speed

In almost any variety of home crafting, power tools make a noticeable difference—most jobs can be done easier, faster, and with more precision than by hand. There are two general categories of power tools—portable and bench-mounted.

Portable Power Tools

Portable tools are not as accurate as bench tools, but their convenience and mobility may easily justify their purchase.

Electric drill is the most versatile of all portable power tools. Hole-drilling is its regular duty, but attachments are available for sanding, polishing, grinding,

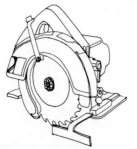

routing, turning, sawing, and many other jobs. Check into the assortment of attachments—you will probably put an electric drill at the top of your tool shopping list.

Electric handsaw is very useful for cutting large sheets of plywood and lengths of standard-sized lumber. It's easy to handle and maneuver—you simply

guide the saw along the line you're cutting. Blade diameters range from $4\frac{1}{2}$ to 12 inches. A special table is available for converting a power handsaw into a tablesaw.

Saber saw is a popular tool because of its ability to make both straight and intricately-curved cuts—and it is priced relatively low. It will cut wood up to 2 inches thick, and blades are available for cutting sheet metal, plastic, and rubber. Attachments include a rip guide

and an angle base. You can easily make cut-outs or do key-hole work by riding

the saw on the tip of its "shoe" and slowly lowering it to cut through.

A router makes smooth, groove-type cuts. It is very handy for making joints—including rabbet, dado, mortise-and-tenon, and dovetail—and it's also useful

for beading and inlaying. Attachments are available for quick conversion into a saber saw, orbital sander, or electric plane.

Orbital sander has a sanding pad that moves in a tiny circle, allowing you to sand either with or across the wood

grain. You can do both heavy and finish sanding, depending upon the coarseness of the abrasive paper you attach.

Vibrator, or reciprocating sander, can also be used for either heavy-duty or

fine finishing work (depending upon the abrasive) but has a pad that moves back and forth in a straight line.

Belt sander must be kept moving with the grain at all times, as the sanding

belt moves in only one direction. It is useful for sanding large, flat surfaces

where you want to remove large quantities of wood rapidly.

Bench-Type Power Tools

For furniture making, there are two bench-type power tools commonly found in the home shop; the table saw and the drill press. The lathe is very handy for turning furniture legs and round pieces, and the jointer precisely smooths edges and faces of boards, but most craftsmen consider both to be more luxury than necessity.

The table saw is extremely useful for accurately cutting both large and small pieces of wood. It is usually equipped with a ripping fence for long, accurate

cuts, and a miter gauge for precise cutting of ends and various angles in shorter pieces. Several accessories are available for special cuts and particular shaping jobs.

Drill press is designed for drilling accurate, uniform holes. Most presses are equipped with stops for easy control of

angle and depth. For projects that require a lot of hole-drilling, a drill press is invaluable. The machine is also handy for mortising and—with attachments—shaping, routing, and drum sanding.

Joining pieces together

When starting on the actual construction of a piece of furniture, the first question the home craftsman should ask himself is, "What is the best way to join the pieces together?" There are many types of joints commonly used in woodworking—some are easy to make, others are not so easy. The ones you decide to use in joining a particular project should depend upon the strength the piece requires, the appearance you wish to achieve, and the work you are willing to do. Don't make joints more complicated than necessary, but be sure they are strong enough to do the job.

When cutting a joint, work carefully to insure a firm, square fit. Always make the cut with the entire saw-kerf on the waste side of the cutting line. Use a sharp saw. A *backsaw*, which has a stiffly-reinforced blade and fine teeth, is best for cutting joints by hand. Jigs and clamps are always helpful for accurate sawing, particularly when making several similar joints.

Unless you plan to disassemble the joint for some reason, always use glue to give it added strength. Don't exclude the use of nails, screws, bolts, and other fasteners.

Lap Joints

Used mainly for joining rails, the lap joint is commonly found joining table and chair legs and supports. The two main types are the *half-lap* and the *cross-lap*. To make a lap joint, mark the width of each board where it is to be joined, and use a saw to cut (on the

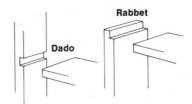

inside of the lines) to half the thickness of each board (or half the thickness of the thinnest board if you're using two different thicknesses). Cut or chisel out the waste wood.

Mortise-and-Tenon Joints

Like the lap joint, mortise-and-tenon is used primarily for joining rails. But

you can also use this type of joint to secure a rail to a surface (such as a

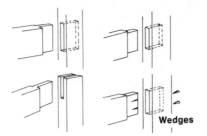

Wedges

piece of plywood). Cut the tenon with a saw. To shape a mortise of matching size, use a router, or drill holes and then chisel out the waste. You might try a mortising attachment available for drill presses. If the tenon doesn't fit snugly, drive one or two small wooden wedges into the end after joining.

Miter Joints

At a corner where visible end grain is undesirable, a miter is often used. The only tools needed to make simple miter joints are a square for marking complimentary angles and a saw for cutting the

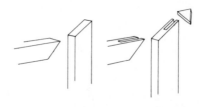

pieces. A miter box is very helpful in guiding a saw to accurately cut angles. Splines or dowels can be inserted in a miter joint to give it strength.

Dado and Rabbet Cuts

The rabbet and dado are commonly used in furniture building—especially for joining cabinet sides, tops, and

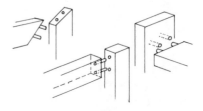

Rabbet

Dado

shelves. Both cuts are easily made with a router or dado-blade assembly on a power saw. You can also make the cuts with a handsaw. To cut a dado by hand, make several cuts in the area to be removed, and chisel out the waste wood.

Using Dowels

Dowels can be used to strengthen almost any type of joint. The ordinary, basic butt joint can be quite strong if dowels are added. To keep holes aligned when making a dowel joint, use dowel pins or a square to mark, and a doweling-jig to drill the holes. If you don't have a doweling-jig, drive two small tacks into end of rails, snip heads off tacks, line up the boards to be

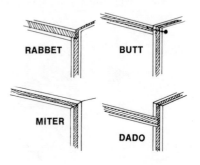

joined, and tap them together. When you remove the tacks, two small holes on each piece will show you where to drill. Score dowels spirally with the corner of a file to permit excess glue to escape when you insert them. If they are difficult to insert, try rounding the ends.

Plywood Joints

Plywood is joined using the miter, butt, rabbet, or dado. Butt joints are practical only when using frame construction or

RABBET   **BUTT**

MITER   **DADO**

¾-inch plywood. If you use thinner plywood, a reinforcing block or nailing strip will make a stronger joint.

Making tabletops

Building a table can be easier than you think if you master a few basic techniques. The suggestions offered here concern making and cutting tabletops. For table-base ideas, see the tables on pages 18-25.

Joining Planks for Tabletops

Most tabletops consist of several boards fastened together in some manner as to form a flat surface. Large planks can be joined either with dowels or with threaded rods plus glue. Long expanding clamps are needed for doweling. If you don't have such clamps, and prefer not to rent them, the planks can be drilled, glued, and tightened together with threaded rods. Two tables with tops laminated in unusual ways (requiring minimum tools) can be seen on pages 23 and 24.

Before joining planks, cut them 1/2 to 1 inch longer than finished length to allow for final squaring and trimming. Lay planks side by side with grain of all planks running in the same direction. Check the end grain of each plank and

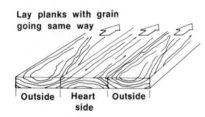

Lay planks with grain going same way

Outside | Heart side | Outside

alternate direction of annual rings to minimize warping.

With planks arranged, number them and mark "face" on upper surface of each. Edges should fit closely.

To join planks with dowels, begin by clamping the first two planks together face to face with edges flush. Mark for

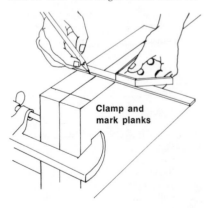

Clamp and mark planks

drill holes as shown, allowing six inches between dowels except at the ends, where dowels should be set about three inches from the trim lines.

Don't attempt drilling using a hand-held drill unless you have a doweling-jig (or at least a square) to guide straight holes—if the holes are not matched exactly, the planks will not fit evenly.

Cut each dowel a fraction shorter than the combined depth of the two holes. Brush edges of planks with glue, allowing some to run into holes. Dip one end

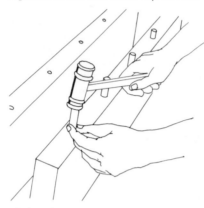

of dowel in glue and drive in. Apply glue to other half of the dowel and drive opposing plank onto the doweled plank with light hammer blows. Place a strip or block of wood on the plank edge to prevent marring.

Clamp all planks together, alternating clamps above and below. Wipe away surplus glue and let stand until dry. (Note: When attaching supporting rails to a finished tabletop, remember that it may shrink across the grain as much as 3/8-inch. Use special tabletop fasteners that allow movement.)

Threaded rods can also be used to join planks. You need a drill bit long enough to drill through the width of the board, and a doweling jig is almost a necessity for boring straight holes. Drill the hole to a slightly larger diameter than that of the threaded rod. Rods should be at least 1/2-inch in diameter.

Mark the planks for drilling in the same way as shown for doweling. Use two threaded rods for any table of less than 5 feet; three rods for tables up to 8 feet.

Where holes pierce outer edges of tabletop, drill larger holes (about 1-inch-diameter) to receive a washer, nut, and wooden plug.

When all holes are drilled, slide rods through planks to check fit. Also check

the length of the rods—if too long, cut them with a hacksaw (leave room to fill edge holes with wooden plugs). Remove rods. Put a washer and nut on one end of each rod, then slide the rods through first end plank. Brush glue generously on the inner edge of the plank and slide second plank onto rods. Continue until all planks are together. Cap the rod at the last plank with a washer and nut, cinching it tight (you will probably need a socket wrench). Glue a wooden plug in the holes at the end of each rod.

Cut table ends when glue is dry, and sand the surface flat.

Cutting a Circular Tabletop

Cutting a circular tabletop is fairly easy using either hand or power tools.

To cut a disc from a single slab of hardwood or plywood, first scribe the circle with a pencil attached by a string or a wood strip (a yardstick will do) to a

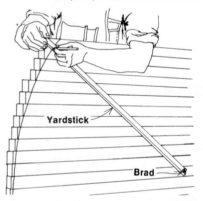

Yardstick

Brad

nail in the center. Cut along the line with a coping saw, saber saw, or band saw; or make a series of straight cuts with a handsaw or bench saw. If you use a saber saw, you can attach it to a wood strip nailed to the center and make your cut without having to scribe it first. Sand the edge smooth.

If you plan to cut a disc from doweled planks, it may be easier to assemble the top first without glue. Scribe the circle and mark the boards, then take it apart and cut the individual planks.

If you use a band saw to cut a very large plank top you will need to support the edge not resting on the saw table. Suspend the top from the ceiling by wire and turnbuckle attached to the center-point. If you wish, rest it on an auxiliary bench, or persuade a helper to hold it while you guide it past the blade.

Drawers...assembling and installing

Some methods for making drawers and runners call for the skill of a professional cabinet maker, but those shown here are both simple and sure.

Drawer Construction

Regardless of the construction method, each drawer will normally require the same number and size of grooves and cuts. By standardizing your procedure, you can repeat the same grooves and cuts for several drawers.

Be sure to cut all pieces exactly, and remember to allow 3/32-inch between drawer and frame, so that the drawer will have room to slide. Use 1/2-inch material for drawer sides and 1/4-inch stock for the drawer bottom.

If you have a power saw (with dado-blade assembly) or a router, the best method is pictured in the top drawing. After adjusting the blade to cut at 1/2-inch width, either rabbet or dado the front of the drawer to fit the sides (depending upon whether you want the drawer front to overlap the sides of the frame). Using the same adjustment, cut dadoes in the sides to fit the back into, and dadoes *along* the sides for the drawer runners. Readjust the blade to 1/4-inch (or make two passes with a regular table-saw blade) to cut grooves about 3/4-inch

up from the lower edge of each side to allow for the drawer bottom. The back can fit flush against the bottom. If you have a router, you can join front, back, and sides with dovetail joints. Check for fit before assembling with glue.

The second drawer shown is best if you don't have a tool that will easily cut dadoes. Again, check for proper fit before starting assembly—you will be using glue to insure rigidity.

Brad and glue a piece of 1/4-inch plywood to the inside of the drawer front. Nail the sides to this. (Instead of the single plywood piece, you could mount a 1/2 by 1/2-inch block inside each of the two front corners with glue and screws.) Nail the back in butt fashion to the inner face of each side. A 1/4 by 1/4-inch strip, nailed around the lower inside perimeter of sides and front, holds the bottom in place. If the drawer is not expected to hold heavy items, nail the bottom flush to the lower edge of each side.

Drawer Guides

A drawer obviously requires a system of guides, to slide in and out on. Side guides are usually all that's needed except for very wide or heavily-loaded drawers. The center slide, while requiring a little more work, helps avoid binding and keeps

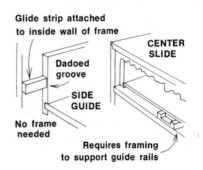

Glide strip attached to inside wall of frame

CENTER SLIDE

Dadoed groove

SIDE GUIDE

No frame needed

Requires framing to support guide rails

drawer centered. For a very smooth-moving drawer, install ball-bearing drawer guides (available at hardware stores).

Locating Wooden Guides

First, prepare the guide strips by drilling three holes in each strip. These should be countersunk so that screws won't protrude past the surface. If you use 1-inch flathead screws, the counterbore should be approximately 3/8-inch. For drawers with sides dadoed to fit runners, you will need one strip for each side; for the other type shown, you will need two.

The location of each glide can be calculated and the glide installed before assembling the frame. But to eliminate the risk of error in calculation, most craftsmen prefer to install the glides *after* the drawers have been assembled. This way you can check the exact location for each pair of glides. Follow this procedure:

Start with the lowest drawer and fit two glides loosely into place in the grooves on the outside surface of each drawer side. (If the drawer isn't grooved, place the glides under the sides.) Set the drawer carefully in place inside the frame. Shim up the drawer front 3/32-inch so that it doesn't rest on the bottom brace, then sight down through the crack at the side of the drawer front. Mark the exact location for each glide on the sides of the frame; then remove the drawer and use the 2-foot square to mark guidelines inside the frame.

Screw the glides into place and fit the drawer back into the frame. If it binds, sand or plane down the glide rail until the drawer slides smoothly and easily. Two bumper strips, nailed and glued to back ends of the glide rails, will allow the drawers to recess about 3/8-inch back from the front edge of the frame. By changing the dimension of these strips, you can make the drawers flush or recess them even further, as you prefer.

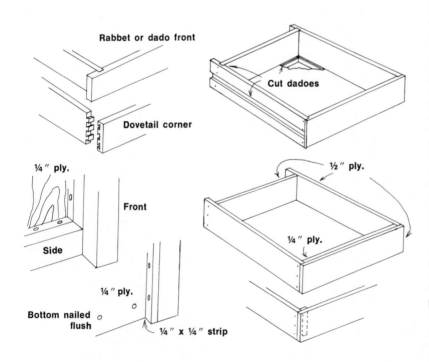

Rabbet or dado front

Cut dadoes

Dovetail corner

1/4" ply.

1/2" ply.

Front

1/4" ply.

Side

1/4" ply.

Bottom nailed flush

1/4" x 1/4" strip

Cabinet doors

Although you can make your own cabinet doors easily enough, you may buy ready-made doors from builders' supply houses—provided your cabinet frames will accept standard sizes. Stock units come in a variety of facings and styles.

When hanging doors, allow for free movement between matching doors (and around hinges). Some carpenters judge the amount of space needed between paired doors by inserting a paper match between them before setting hinges.

Hinged Doors

Hinged doors, the standard for cabinets, are of two types: flush or lip. Flush doors give uniform appearance to a series of units, and are often preferred for ease of installation (with butt hinges). They can be easily recessed, or attached so that they project slightly. They are, however, unpopular with some craftsmen because they tend to amplify any errors; when the cabinet settles or hinges begin to sag, flush doors may complicate the problem by jamming against the cabinet frame or showing open space along door edges.

Lip edges not only offer a pleasant appearance, but also help cover errors. By rabbeting a ¼-inch or ⅜-inch lip, plus a ⅛-inch clearance around the cabinet opening, you can make sure that the fit will remain reasonably true and minor sags unnoticeable.

Hinges and latches, in many ways, determine the success of the door. Use hinges that will support the full weight of the door and are strong enough to open and close easily without sagging or sticking. You can purchase hinges that enhance the beauty of the cabinetwork, others that remain completely concealed when the door is closed. A few extra dollars invested in hinges destined for often-used cabinets may eliminate troubles and forestall early replacement.

There are also several types and styles of latches on the market, each featuring a different "trap." Solid types are best for cabinets subject to constant use—these are least likely to loosen or bend and are not dependent on strict alignment to function properly.

Sliding Doors

Sliding doors on cabinets and closets offer a number of advantages over the hinged type. They may be moved aside quickly, they take up minimum space, offer a clean surface, and—on better hardware—roll quietly and effortlessly.

Their main disadvantage is that only half the cabinet can be opened at once when overlapping doors are used. Poorly-constructed doors and tracks may stick, make noise, or jam. Newer types of plastic and fiber tracks help prevent the last difficulty, but if the door sags or bows it will stick in any type of track.

The simplest and most inexpensive sliding door is a thin panel that slides between two wooden stops. The panel can be of tempered hardboard, plywood, glass, or plastic. Use ¼" round as stops, and cut your panels to fit the opening with a ⅟₁₆-inch clearance for easy sliding. Sand the edges of the panels and soap the slots.

If you want completely closed storage, you will need by-passing panels. This calls for three stops—one in the center

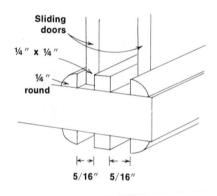

Sliding doors
¼" x ¼"
¼" round
5/16"   5/16"

and one on each side. Use a ¼-inch-square strip at the center and ¼" round on the sides.

If you have a power saw with dado-blade assembly, you can dispense with the stops (which must be nailed or glued) and cut channels directly into cabinet shelves.

A good channel depth for ¾-inch shelving is ³⁄₁₆-inch at the top and bot-

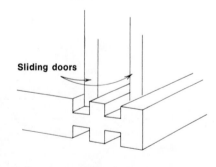

Sliding doors

tom. Cut the channel ⅟₁₆-inch wider than the panel, add ⁵⁄₁₆-inch to the height of the opening, and you have the proper height for your sliding panels (this leaves ⅟₁₆-inch clearance for easy sliding).

If you want removable panels, cut down the panel height slightly so you get just a ⅟₁₆-inch "bite" at the top channel. This will give enough clearance to permit lifting out the panels. A deeper top channel will serve the same purpose, if you prefer.

Fiber channels are sometimes used for sliding doors. The bone-hard material gives a much smoother ride than wood-on-wood. You can buy either single or double track varieties.

The single-track style has a single runner that fits into a groove on the cabinet shelf or closet floor. Fiber shoes, dadoed into the bottom of the doors, glide along

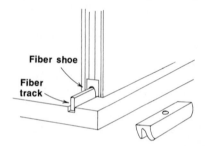

Fiber shoe
Fiber track

this runner. Since the runner causes a ridge in the shelf or floor, you can reverse the system: closely space shoes in the floor, and dado the runner (end

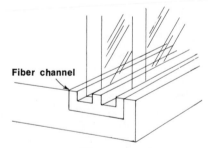

Fiber channel

should be beveled) into the door.

Double channels of molded fiber have been developed for glass sliding doors. You dado the channels into the shelf. Glass does not need to be beveled, for the bottom of the channel is curved up to insure a minimum of bearing surface.

At the top of the door, you can use the same channels inverted (add wood stops), or you can cut dadoed grooves. With glass panels, allow enough clearance at the top so you can push them up and remove for cleaning.

Standard furniture dimensions

The home craftsman can modify many of the plans in this book (as well as others) to fit his particular needs. You may, in fact, use some of the plans as basic ideas for creating totally new designs. If you do make changes, be sure that parts and joints are strong enough to take everyday use. Also, remember that dimensions must be comfortable and convenient.

Here are a few general tips to aid you in building properly-sized furniture.

Table sizes depend on intended location and vary according to their function and the number of people to be seated at one time. The chart below gives some of the standard dimensions of rectangular tables.

	Height	Width	Length
Dining	29-30	36-40	56-62
		38-48	72-79
Breakfast	29-30	25-30	30-45
		35-41	48-58
Coffee	12-18	16½-17	32½-35½
		19-22	36-44
		22-32	48-56
		22-38	63-79

Table legs should not be set at an angle that will reduce their strength or trip passersby.

Chair design can be quite tricky. The beginner would do well to follow printed plans closely. A chair must be attractive, comfortable, and strong enough to withstand heavy use. Height from floor to top of seat is usually about 15 to 18 inches—in order to comfortably support the thigh. The seat should have a slight backward tilt of about 3 inches, and the back posts should slant rearward from 2 to 4 inches. Depth of the seat normally ranges from 15 to 21 inches, depending upon the type of chair. The top slat should support the back just below the shoulder blades (about 18 to 20 inches above the seat).

Desk surfaces should have a minimum area of 14 by 22 inches, not including typewriter space. A typewriter can be kept on top of a desk, but if you want to store it inside the desk, allow an area 20 inches deep, 22 inches wide, and 12 inches high for a standard model. A space 16 inches deep, 16 inches wide, and 10 inches high will house a portable typewriter.

An average writing desk is 30 inches high, but a typewriter should sit 3 inches lower. Kneehole dimensions are important; for comfort, the kneehole should be about 21 inches deep, 25 inches high, and 22 inches wide.

Bookshelf lengths can be figured by estimating 8 to 10 average-sized books to each running foot of shelf. Nine inches of height will accommodate most books, and one or two shelves with a 12-inch clearance will hold the larger sizes. A good depth for most bookshelves is 10 inches (see page 26).

Shelving units designed to hold things other than books (such as stereo components) will have varying dimensions according to the objects' sizes and the space required to use them.

If you house stereo components in a closed compartment, consider ventilation. Transistorized amplifiers and tuners don't build up heat, but those with tubes do—and require ventilation.

Chests of drawers will vary in height from 36 to 54 inches. The depth should be 18 to 21 inches. For a single-drawer-wide chest, widths run from 28 to 36 inches.

Most beds have standard lengths of 78 to 80 inches. Heights are 22 to 24 inches (with the mattress in place). Widths of single beds are 36 to 42 inches, a double bed is 54 inches, "queen-sized" is 60 inches, and "king-sized" is 72 inches (sometimes as wide as 78 inches).

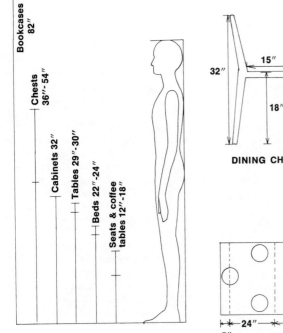

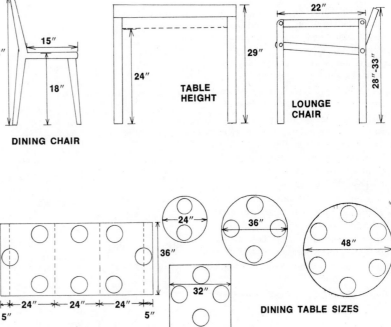

Choosing and applying the finish

Once you have completed the construction of a piece of furniture, you should decide on the type of finish you will give the wood. The most suitable finish depends on two considerations: how tough a surface you want and the type of wood you are using.

Before applying your selected finish to an entire project, try it out on the underside or on a scrap of the same type wood. You'll often have to experiment with finishes in order to achieve a uniformly rich appearance over the entire project since many of those shown in this book are made from a combination of woods.

Protective Finishes

Furniture wood must be protected. It is too easily soiled or damaged if left in its natural state. Wax, shellac, lacquer, varnish, penetrating resin, and oil are all transparent protective finishes that help preserve the natural color of wood.

Waxing. Wax gives a soft, lustrous gloss but it protects wood only from dirt discoloration. First, apply a thinned coat of shellac or resin sealer. Then sand lightly and follow with at least three coats of paste wax, buffed after each application.

Shellac. Shellac gives a hard, glossy surface, but doesn't provide a very durable coating. For this reason, it's not recommended for furniture that will be subjected to hard wear. It is a fine finish for giving richness to many medium and dark cabinet woods.

Its lack of durability calls for frequent retouching with alcohol or new shellac. It is soluble in many common household liquids—including thinners, alcohol, ammonia, soaps, detergents, even hard water. Don't use shellac on teak, ebony, or cedar; it's not compatible with these woods.

Purchase shellac fresh—it deteriorates in storage. To use it, thin two parts liquid shellac with one part denatured alcohol.

First smooth the wood. Both staining and filling the wood are optional but often desirable. Then use a fully-loaded brush to apply shellac with a slow, smooth-flowing motion (overlapping adjoining strokes) to develop a clean, even film.

Allow the first coat to dry for 1 or 2 hours, sand with 180 to 220-grit abrasive, and follow same procedures for second and third coats. If you plan to wax the surface, wait 24 hours after the last application. Then apply hard paste wax, and buff.

Lacquer. Speedy application and good surface protection are characteristic of lacquer. Most lacquers dry fast enough to be impervious to dust in 3 minutes.

There are types available for both spraying and brushing. Brush types have a retardant to keep them from drying too fast. When using brush lacquer, you must wait for each coat to dry. Each new coat softens the one beneath; therefore work fast, keep the brush loaded, and draw it over the surface only once. Always brush with the wood grain. Final sanding and rubbing will smooth out rough spots.

If you spray, use the spray gun like a brush, working the length or width of the surface with each stroke. Hold the gun 6 to 10 inches from working surface, draw it slowly back and forth in even paths. Permit a slight overlap. Spray legs and sides first.

Five or six sprayed coats are adequate —any more may crack. Allow four hours drying time between coats. For best finish, apply three coats, let surface dry for 48 hours, rub with 4/0 steel wool, then apply remaining coats. Allow to dry for another 48 hours, then give it a final sanding and rubbing.

Varnish. The most durable and protective of all clear, on-the-surface finishes, modern varnishes produce a tough finish that is heat, abrasion, impact, chemical, alcohol, and water resistant.

Most are synthetics—they can be chemically tailored to specific jobs. Also, they are easier to apply, longer lasting, and produce better surfaces than the older natural oil-resin finishes.

Simply apply evenly on a clean surface, and let dry thoroughly before recoating. Varnishes usually require a long drying time—dust is a real problem. So close all windows and apply varnish in a dust-free room. Scuff carefully between coats with 4/0 steel wool and rub the final coat with FFF pumice sprinkled on a thin layer of rubbing oil, using a felt pad. Remove stray dust particles with a sliver of wood.

A day or two after the final rub, you can apply a hard paste wax to the surface to preserve the glossy finish.

Penetrating resin. This type of finish is ideal for many furniture projects. Wood grain and figure are enhanced by a slight darkening, yet the wood does not appear to be under glass. It is easy to apply, fast drying, tough, and resilient. No filler is required when using penetrating resin—the finish soaks into the surface of the wood, using the wood structure as a fibrous filler.

Apply enough of the resin to keep a clean surface wet for at least half an hour. At the end of this wet (or soak) period, wipe the surface clear with a lint-free cloth. Second and third soaks, if they can be absorbed by the wood, will make a harder surface. To repair a scratched or marred surface, merely apply more resin to the blemishes.

Oiling. Boiled linseed oil, properly applied, will not only seal wood but provide a durable finish. Apply in thin coats while warm, allowing each coat to dry for 48 hours and rubbing with fine sandpaper between coats. Professionals use 6 to 12 coats.

Newer Danish oils are wiped on with a rag quite easily. Spread a generous coat on the wood, let it stand 1 hour, wipe off the excess, and let dry overnight.

Stain Finishes

Wood is stained to emphasize grain and natural figure. Many professionals use stain when wood has little natural beauty of color or graining. Most stains give the wood surface little or no protection, so you may want to use a protective finish as well.

For proper staining, the wood surface must be uniformly smooth, clean, and free of any old finish or wax. Try to work on surfaces horizontally; when you must work on a vertical surface, work from the bottom up with continuous edge-to-edge strokes paralleling the grain to minimize drips and overlap marks.

Water stains give a clear, sharp tone with deep penetration. They have the broadest range of brilliant, warm-toned colors. Their disadvantage is that they raise the grain and require at least 24 hours drying time.

Spirit (alcohol) stains penetrate well, but are slightly less permanent, extremely fast drying, and generally cooler in tone than water dyes. Clean rags make good applicators.

Non-grain-raising stains ("N.G.R." stains) can be either water or spirit stains with non-grain-raising solvents used. They are usually faster-drying than water stains and less difficult to use than spirit stains. They penetrate deeply, are light-fast, dry quickly, and are easy to apply with either brush or rag. A rag gives more even tone; a brush works well on small areas. Uneven finish can be cured by wiping with a rag dipped in special stain thinner. Non-grain-raising stains will bleed through finish coats unless sealed with wash coat of shellac. Drying time is about 4 hours.

Pigmented wiping stains, very much like thin paints, have ground pigments suspended in a vehicle. They are used to accentuate the grain pattern by color fill-in of the open pores, to mask the natural grain pattern in favor of an over-all color, or to simulate another wood.

They may be easily applied with brush, and should be wiped with clean rag soon after application. The longer you delay wiping, the stronger the color. They do not raise wood grain or affect finishing coats.

Fillers

Fillers allow you to give a smooth finish to woods with uneven grains and pores. As purchased, they must be thinned with turpentine or other manufacturer-recommended thinner.

Apply with a stiff brush, working filler well into the grain. When the surface appears dull, wipe across the grain with a piece of burlap. Allow the filled surface to harden for 24 hours before giving it a light sanding.

Before filling the wood, you may want to apply a wash coat of thin shellac to prevent filler from staining the wood and to keep stains from seeping into the filler. Do not use fillers over a wax finish.

How to Finish Woods

Here are some of the most commonly used furniture woods with suggested finishes for each. With the materials described above and the rules described here, you can work out many finishes of your own.

Walnut. Hard and porous, walnut always requires a filler for a smooth finish. However, if you wish the texture to show, eliminate the filler.

For a natural finish, mix natural wood filler with a little burnt umber. Fill the wood, sand lightly, and finish with two coats of water-white lacquer.

For an antique gray bleached finish, first bleach the wood (use any commercial bleach available for woods), sand until the natural color shows, then use a gray filler. Finish with a coat of lacquer or varnish.

For a stain finish, apply the stain, fill the surface of the wood with a wood filler that matches the stain, and finish with varnish or lacquer.

Mahogany. There are a number of varieties and grades of mahogany. The most common is Philippine mahogany, which is softer than other varieties, spongy in texture, and large-pored. All require a filler for a smooth surface.

Oil or wax produces the best natural finish.

Much modern furniture is made of bleached mahogany. Bleach, wash thoroughly with water, and sand until the natural pink of the wood shows through. Fill with a natural wood filler, and finish with clear lacquer.

Mahogany is stained more often than it is left natural. Apply the stain, fill, and finish with varnish or lacquer.

Oak. Strong and durable, oak has large pores that require two coats of filler for a smooth finish.

A natural finish requires filler and a water-white lacquer finish. To soften the yellow cast, use a slightly gray filler.

Two of the most commonly used stain finishes are golden oak and fumed oak. Golden oak may be achieved by applying golden oak stain, filling with a light brown filler, and finishing with varnish or lacquer. The resulting color will be yellow with dark brown filled grain.

Fumed oak produces an orange-brown color similar to the color in most oak hardwood floors. True fumed oak is produced by exposing the wood to ammonia fumes. No task for an amateur, it can be duplicated by applying Adam brown stain, then a dark brown filler. Sand, then finish with varnish or lacquer.

A similar but darker finish, like early English oak, is obtained by mixing Adam brown with about 1/10 part black stain. Apply a wash coat of shellac, fill

with black filler, finish with varnish or lacquer.

Maple, Birch, Gum. These woods have enough characteristics in common that their finishes may be considered together. Maple and birch are very hard, non-porous woods. Gum is non-porous, but is not as hard. It is usually darker than either maple or birch and must be bleached in order to obtain as light a finish. Maple and birch are rarely bleached. None of these woods requires a filler.

Any of the natural finishes work well on any of these woods. Gum has less character than either of the other two and usually is used to imitate some of the more expensive woods.

All of these woods take stains well. You can produce many of the traditional period furniture colors on any of them. Before applying the stain, give these woods a wash coat of shellac, made by thinning one part of white shellac with five parts of alcohol. Then stain and finish with varnish or lacquer.

Pine. About the only softwood that has a very high value in furniture, pine is a close-grained wood that requires no filler.

To finish pine in a nearly natural color, apply a coat of lacquer sanding sealer, sand thoroughly, and finish with lacquer or varnish.

Pine will take all of the stains that work well on maple, birch, and gum. If you intend to disguise it with a stain, it is a good idea to apply a wash coat of shellac before staining, sand well, stain, apply lacquer sanding sealer, sand, and lacquer.

Teak. Very porous, quite hard, and very durable, teak requires two applications of filler to achieve a glass-smooth finish. If you wish to retain some of the porous texture of the wood, use only one application.

Since teak is about the color of nutmeg, it is rarely bleached. When it becomes wet, fibers of the wood swell, making the surface very rough. To eliminate the possibility of a rough surface finish, sponge the wood with hot water before you apply any finish. Allow the surface to dry, and then sand with No. 7/0 sandpaper. Dust or vacuum thoroughly. Then apply your finish materials.

Never use shellac or any other sealer on teak. The natural oils of the wood are not compatible with shellac gums.

For a natural finish, use water-white lacquer or oil.

PHOTO CREDITS